Praise for the Innocent Class

The Innocent Classroom has reaffirmed my philosophy as a teacher, an administrator, a mom, and a person. I have always felt that strong and genuine relationships with my students were the precursor to future success. It is a fact of life that as educators, we all feel the constant pressure of getting through the curriculum, worrying about standardized test scores, and making AYP. Alexs Pate's passion for fostering children's innocence focuses on creating a school community that prioritizes building, advocating for, and protecting the "good" of each of our children. While I could cite research on the correlation between positive student-teacher relationships and increased student achievement, effort, and personal growth, the day-to-day experiences of the heart are proof enough for me. You, our children, and I will *all* work harder and achieve more when we know we are valued for our unique "goods" that drive us in all that we do. The Innocent Classroom brings us back to nurturing the soul and heart. With this vital component, our children will succeed—both academically and emotionally. The Innocent Classroom has made me reflect, go deeper, and see what makes each child (and adult) truly unique. I appreciate and applaud Alexs Pate for his dedication in helping all of us find and value the true human spirit within us.

—Elementary school assistant principal and former classroom teacher,
Omaha, Nebraska

I've never seen a practice or a program that has changed hearts and minds so fast. We haven't even finished our training, but there's been an immediate culture shift.

—K–8 school principal, St. Cloud, Minnesota

It works. Kids will do things for teachers they love. Our graduation rate has gone up. We are one of the highest graduation-rate growers over the last five years in the entire state of Minnesota and in the metro area. The last few years, we've had about 16-point growth, and we have also made very large gains with all groups within our district. We have closed gaps between our Latino and white students. We have closed gaps between black and white students, our ELL and non-ELL students, and our special ed and non-special ed students.

—Superintendent, suburban Minneapolis public school district

With Innocent Classroom, you end up with kids who care about each other, kids who can be flexible when you need to change something, kids who can be patient if you are struggling with technology, kids who will do anything for the greater good. When I even start to ask, "Is there someone who could . . . ?" 15 hands go up because they want to help. When you lead with finding innocence, kids who screamed and ran the halls or needed a one-on-one adult at other schools become the stars of your class. When you lead with finding innocence, you get higher test scores . . . five years in a row.

—Teacher, Lucy Craft Laney Community School, Minneapolis

THE
INNOCENT
CLASSROOM

ASCD MEMBER BOOK

Many ASCD members received this book as a
member benefit upon its initial release.

Learn more at: **www.ascd.org/memberbooks**

THE INNOCENT CLASSROOM

Dismantling **Racial Bias**
to Support Students of Color

ALEXS PATE

Alexandria, Virginia USA

1703 N. Beauregard St. • Alexandria, VA 22311-1714 USA
Phone: 800-933-2723 or 703-578-9600 • Fax: 703-575-5400
Website: www.ascd.org • E-mail: member@ascd.org
Author guidelines: www.ascd.org/write

Ranjit Sidhu, *CEO & Executive Director;* Stefani Roth, *Publisher;* Genny Ostertag, *Director, Content Acquisitions;* Allison Scott, *Acquisitions Editor;* Julie Houtz, *Director, Book Editing & Production;* Miriam Calderone, *Editor;* Judi Connelly, *Senior Art Director;* Melissa Johnston, *Graphic Designer;* Keith Demmons, *Senior Production Designer;* Kelly Marshall, *Manager, Production Services;* Shajuan Martin, *E-Publishing Specialist*

All web links in this book are correct as of the publication date below but may have become inactive or otherwise modified since that time. If you notice a deactivated or changed link, please e-mail books@ascd.org with the words "Link Update" in the subject line. In your message, please specify the web link, the book title, and the page number on which the link appears.

PAPERBACK ISBN: 978-1-4166-2933-7   ASCD product #120025
PDF E-BOOK ISBN: 978-1-4166-2935-1; see Books in Print for other formats.
Quantity discounts are available: e-mail programteam@ascd.org or call 800-933-2723, ext. 5773, or 703-575-5773. For desk copies, go to www.ascd.org/deskcopy.

ASCD Member Book No. FY20-9 (Aug 2020 P). ASCD Member Books mail to Premium (P), Select (S), and Institutional Plus (I+) members on this schedule: Jan, PSI+; Feb, P; Apr, PSI+; May, P; Jul, PSI+; Aug, P; Sep, PSI+; Nov, PSI+; Dec, P. For current details on membership, see www.ascd.org/membership.

Library of Congress Cataloging-in-Publication Data

Names: Pate, Alexs D., 1950- author.
Title: The innocent classroom : dismantling racial bias to support students of color / Alexs Pate.
Description: Alexandria, Virginia : ASCD, [2020] | Includes bibliographical references and index.
Identifiers: LCCN 2020017513 (print) | LCCN 2020017514 (ebook) | ISBN 9781416629337 (paperback) | ISBN 9781416629351 (pdf)
Subjects: LCSH: African Americans--Education. | Stereotypes (Social psychology)--United States. | Discrimination in education--United States--Prevention. | Innocent Classroom (Workshop)
Classification: LCC LC2717 .P38 2020 (print) | LCC LC2717 (ebook) | DDC 371.829/96073--dc23
LC record available at https://lccn.loc.gov/2020017513
LC ebook record available at https://lccn.loc.gov/2020017514

29 28 27 26 25 24 23 22 21 20   1 2 3 4 5 6 7 8 9 10 11 12

For my daughter Sxela, her friends, and children everywhere,
and the teachers and parents who work hard to save them

THE INNOCENT CLASSROOM

Dismantling **Racial Bias** to Support Students of Color

Acknowledgments

The concept of the Innocent Classroom sprang from a belief. So many people had to share in that belief for it to evolve, and many more have had to engage and implement it for that belief to become real. My deepest thanks to everyone who has supported this work. I want to especially thank Dr. Matthew Brandt for his initial encouragement and support and Jess Annabelle, who has done the impossible to ensure our success.

My thanks also to all the folks who have been deeply engaged in this effort, including Joseph Leadley, Julian Condie, Adebisi Wilson, Jaimee Wolcott, Fallon Gleason, Lar'Ranz Guider, Iman Hassan, Sami Saltzman, David Mura, J. Otis Powell, June Yoshinari Davis, Damu McCoy, Tom Nelson, Scott Erickson, Craig Green, Tai Coleman, Rob Johnson, Tony Orange, Tameika Williams, Avigdor Edminster, Chris Mangold, Chad Hancock, and Alexandria Delcourt.

I would like to thank the Minnesota Humanities Center for giving me the opportunity to conceptualize and demonstrate the Innocent Classroom training, as well as the Sherwood Foundation and other funders who have supported the districts and schools engaged in this work. I particularly want to thank the early adopters, including Omaha Public Schools, Saint Paul Public Schools, Northside Achievement Zone, Equity Alliance MN, South Saint Paul School

District, NECC Early Childhood, Saint Paul Promise Neighborhood, Friendship Academy, Mounds View Public Schools, Minneapolis Public Schools, Richfield Public Schools, and the schools we've worked in in Reno, Nevada; San Jose, California; Providence, Rhode Island; Valley View, Illinois; and Milwaukee and Racine, Wisconsin, for the opportunity to engage their educators. Without the opportunity to work in these environments, we wouldn't have the data to prove the efficacy of our approach.

Last, I want to personally thank Bob Coughlan, Jerry Bexten, Katie Weitz, Dr. David O'Fallon, Casey DeMarais, Sondra Samuels, Dr. Eric Jolly, Ann Mulholland, Jerry Timian, Dr. Nora Murphy, Dr. Eleanor Coleman, Kevin Lindsey, Dr. SooJin Pate, Kate Gipp, Jennifer Tonko, Rose McGee, Dr. Omawale Akintunde, Dr. Tommy Watson, Julianne Schwietz, Eden Bart, Jimmie Johnson, Janice Gilmore, Jeff Hom, Jonah Edelman, Dr. Dan Saltzman, Mary Bussman, Dr. Susan Sencer, Michael Thomas, Michelle Bierman, Nicole Bates, Steve Unowsky, Leadriane Roby, Dr. Jennifer Mueller, Jay Salter, Charvez Russel, Nell Collier, Amy Kellogg, Sherida Britt, Patricia Stockland, Gyanni Scott, Alexs Thompson, and, especially, Rachel Voller. Thanks also to ASCD, especially Allison Scott and Miriam Calderone.

Preface

When I think of children of color, in my head, in my dreams—when their images are disconnected from cold reality—they appear as I see or saw myself as a child. Curious. Energetic. Smart. Brilliant, even. Innocent. Yes: *innocent.* Young, gifted, and innocent.

In the beginning, I did not set out on a journey to create a professional development program for teachers. I simply began to meditate on what I had absorbed from what popular culture had to say about me. The truth was that no matter how I saw myself, I always expected I was being seen in a different way, a fragmented sensation referred to by W. E. B. Du Bois as "double consciousness." It is a complex truth, but suffice it to say that I never felt that the world outside my family and friends had the slightest idea of who I was.

I have lived much of my life as a writer. A poet. An artist. And the art I made, the poems and novels I wrote, were mostly about humanizing myself and the people I met on my journey. I was entangled in a reality in which I was always seen through a filter of stereotypes. This affected my life in myriad ways. I have no doubt that negative stereotypes settled into my unconscious and shaped my behavior. I found myself waiting for disaster and feeling a nearly constant sense of what I'm calling, in this context, guilt. The stereotypes that popular culture had constructed about me had gradually led me to act, more often than not, as though they were true. My instinctive reaction to events and people around me seemed more like a programmed response than how I might actually be feeling.

I wanted to be free of that way of being. So I began a yearslong meditation, one that continues to this day, to eliminate that guilt and its relationship to how I lived and its influence on the decisions I made. I wanted to remove that feeling of unspecified culpability, of being a conspirator in my own limitations—to put it simply, my sense of guilt.

As I learned more about the work I was doing, I rediscovered Aristotle (1996) and his definition of *good*: "that for which all else is done." As I thought about how to render myself innocent, I began to meditate on my own good. I wasn't what was rumored. I was not a negative representation of myself. I discovered that I could escape the bonds of negative stereotypes by embracing my *good*.

As it happened, around the time I was engaged in this exploration of my own good, I found myself in a meeting with a group of people who were discussing cultural proficiency training for educators. At the end of that meeting, I mentioned the essay I was writing called "Revolutionary Innocence." The responses I received relayed intense curiosity: *What did I mean? How was I going about this effort to free myself? Did I think many children of color were affected by this?* And so on. From that moment, I knew I had to follow my theory about negative stereotypes and guilt to some conclusion.

With the encouragement of Dr. Matthew Brandt (then vice president of the Minnesota Humanities Center and now vice president of my company, Innocent Technologies LLC) and support from a major regional foundation, I set out to create a program of engagement for educators to help their students disconnect from negative stereotypes and recognize their teachers as people who were there to help them in their academic careers, from kindergarten through high school graduation.

The first workshop of the Innocent Classroom in 2012 was met with strong support from the educators in the room. In the ensuing sessions, we've learned that using innocence as a goal for every child in a classroom can have a dramatic impact on both their behavior and their academic engagement. That innocence can function as a tool of liberation for our children—and for teachers, as well.

I gradually became immersed in a process that every day seemed less theoretical and more like a concrete answer to what has been called the "achievement gap." Teachers began talking about how they were changing, how they felt more committed to the children they taught, and how they could see their humanity more clearly.

This led me to see our educators differently. Yes, their jobs are hard, they are underpaid, and their working conditions are often subpar, but they stand before their students in spite of those conditions and, in the main, are willing and able to educate our children. Now I also see them as a liberating force. Properly trained and engaged with our children, they can lead students away from the bondage of negative images, narratives, and iconography toward an environment in which they are free to be curious and active learners.

In the construction and implementation of the Innocent Classroom, together with the educators we have worked with, we have learned how to create empathy where very little existed. We have learned that identifying a child's good begins with understanding what drives and motivates them. We have learned that telling a child that you can see their good makes it possible for them to choose to live out of that good.

We have learned, too, that when a child believes you, when they trust that you do indeed see their good, you are in fact encouraging them to embrace their innocence. And the more their innocence is engaged, the more likely they are to shed the weight of negative stereotypes that marginalize them and minimize their educational attainment. They can be better students.

The Innocent Classroom is not a cultural competency or proficiency program. Those programs have their place, but the Innocent Classroom goes beyond that. The only new knowledge required in this approach is that of the individual child, as opposed to knowledge of children's aggregated cultural histories that might help explain the problem but almost never provides an individualized solution to academic failure. Indeed, we have become a culture that spends most of its time describing the problems in public education. The Innocent

Classroom is solution based. What's more, it puts the strategic capacity in the hands of teachers.

It is past time for us to stop trying to *manage* our children. Whatever form that approach takes, it seems to create disparate outcomes. Rather, it is time to *understand* our children and help them come to believe that they can exist outside any stereotypical image or idea they have been led to believe about themselves.

All we ask is that educators begin this work with the belief that our children can be brilliant and powerful learners who have been weighed down by so many burdens and barriers that they can't see who is there for them and who is just there. To some children, we're all just there.

When I was developing the Innocent Classroom, I wanted to get video testimony from mothers describing how they felt on the day they gave birth: what did they remember about what they had hoped for their newborn? Do you know why I wanted to record that testimony? Think about it this way: in our training, when we ask educators to explain what America tells them about who their students are—who children of color are—the answer is fundamentally different. Dramatically different from what their mothers had hoped for upon their birth.

Perhaps we have come to the end of an age. Public education—in the sense that schools crowd hundreds of students into rooms that are sorted by age and expect them to learn what is being taught—is dying fast. Our system's inability to reach children of color may, in fact, be its last rasping breath.

If we go about it the right way, this ineffective system can give way to one that reflects a more enlightened understanding of who the children are who sit uneasily at their desks. Maybe this is the dawn of a new age in public education: the age of the child. The individual child. The innocent child.

Introduction

One day last spring, as I walked out of my house to run some errands, I was immediately hit by an overwhelming sense of sadness. It was such a bright, wondrous day, and the heavy sweet smell of blooming lilacs swirled around me. It should have made me happy, but instead, the sunlight careening off the buildings and the fresh smell of spring transported me into the past. And no matter how bucolic or sunswept my memories of the past may be, they almost always leave me sad.

I grew up in North Philadelphia, not far from the Philadelphia Zoo, in a neighborhood of working-class black folks who had grabbed on to the promise of the American Dream and were barely holding on. But on my street, the sun did shine, and Saturdays were full of purposeful activities like cleaning the house and turning the garden hose on the cement sidewalk in front of the house.

As a child, I loved pickles. Dill, kosher, hot, sweet, sour, or sweet and sour, it didn't matter. Even thinking about it now brings a rush of saliva to my mouth. I attended an elementary school a block and a half from my house, and I'd always run home at lunchtime, eat the wholesome food my mother prepared (usually a sandwich and a bowl of soup), and then do or say whatever I had to in order to get out of the house. And with the remaining 15 or 20 minutes I had before the afternoon bell rang, I would set out for Little John's.

Little John's was one of those idiosyncratic little stores one can always find in the inner city that carry an astonishing variety of goods—from penny candy to staples, bread to balloons—in a space barely large enough for 10 people to stand without touching. But Little John's was unusual in that it was a corner store that was actually located in the middle of the block. For the life of me, I can't quite figure out how John had accomplished such a feat. I remember that as you approached the store, you'd be confronted by a makeshift enclosed wooden stairway that jutted straight out of the block of row houses. It would almost stop you from walking unimpeded down the street, driving you to wonder what lay behind this odd edifice.

You must understand that in many of Philadelphia's inner-city neighborhoods, so many of the houses are exactly the same, conjoined like a series of train cars being pulled toward the Delaware River, depending almost entirely on the creative and financial resources of the residents to distinguish them from one another. So Little John's was a small wonder. And inside Little John's there was always a barrel full of pungent brine. And swimming in that brine were the largest dang dill pickles you'd ever seen—bigger than any pickles I've seen since. And it wasn't just that they were big; they were fully pickled, so thoroughly saturated that the first bite would make you purse your lips in a tight, vinegared clinch. For a quarter, I would dive into that barrel and spear my catch. Then I'd go back to school, obviously unconcerned with the damage that the pickle might do to my natural cologne. I remember walking out of Little John's with this big pickle and literally skipping up the street. Skipping, I tell you. And in this memory, the sun fanned brilliant light all around, and the bricks were a vivid red, and the asphalt was the deepest black . . . and I was just so happy.

I relay this memory to prove that I was once innocent. Only someone who is without guilt can skip. The slightest weight of guilt will take the skip out of your gait. On this day, there were no suspicious eyes on me. No sense of outsiderness, of being a demon or a criminal. I was just the happiest little black boy, eating my dill pickle and tra-la-la-ing to school.

You may think that the innocence of a child is self-evident. Yet in some strange but undeniable way, our culture robs children of color and most other marginalized children of a reasonable chance to know and experience what I am calling innocence. This void of knowledge and experience of feeling innocent, when combined with other societal and economic issues, often results in children feeling an attitude of apathy or even aversion to authority and to the idea that they can ever be anything but "guilty." It is a destiny of sorts—but it doesn't have to be that way.

The Importance of Innocence

When our children were born, they were free. Undamaged. They opened their eyes to a horizon with no limits. At birth, they knew nothing about the world they were born into.

Unfortunately, the world already had a plan for them. Think about how the media portrays them. Think of the stereotypes about them that fly through the air. Children of color are being held in virtual bondage to the negative stereotypes that our culture has developed and perpetuated about them. These stereotypes define our children as threatening, violent, criminal, poor, and academically disengaged, and they are internalized by many children as guilt before they even enter the school door. For many children, these stereotypes actually become a script that influences their behavior and inhibits their ability to be engaged learners. This script is the reason for the achievement gap and other disparities of the education system.

The Challenge: Negative Stereotypes and Guilt

The damage that negative stereotyping does to our children is massive and wide-ranging. A study by McKown and Strambler (2009) found the following:

> Between ages 5 and 11 . . . children become aware that many people believe stereotypes, including stereotypes about academic ability (for example, how intelligent certain racial and ethnic groups are). When children become aware of these types of bias about their own racial or ethnic group, it can affect how they respond to everyday situations,

ranging from interacting with others to taking tests. (Society for Research in Child Development, 2009, para. 4)

I believe that negative narratives are internalized as guilt in the bodies of our children. And when this happens, the lingering innocence is stolen right out of their lives, maybe forever. They are trapped. We all are. We are all victims in this reality where the bad stories about us dictate how people see us.

Children of color are curious and powerful human beings who are enmeshed in a system that has marked them and labeled them. Many of them don't get a chance to choose who they are; they are told who they are by what they see in film and on television, by what they hear in music, by the stories told about them. So many of us, and so many of our children, are lost to these images and stories that have been constructed and interpreted by those who have not taken the time to know us but who need a way to distinguish themselves from us to validate their own existence or, even worse, their superiority.

Thus, when children of color enter school, they bring with them a host of burdens. Most of these burdens aren't easily identifiable, because they have been bestowed in a way that is completely unnoticed. The children aren't aware they are dragging weights around, and their teachers are likely to be oblivious or, worse, to fear calling attention to them. These burdens are unceremoniously dumped on them by the machinations of our society. The students, their parents, their community, and their teachers may believe what the dominant culture has said about them.

The lack of diversity within the ranks of public schools has exacerbated this reality. If, according to one report, in 2015–2016, "about 80 percent of public school teachers were White, 9 percent were Hispanic, 7 percent were Black, 2 percent were Asian, and 1 percent were of two or more races" (National Center for Education Statistics, 2018, para. 3), we must maximize our effort to humanize our children of color.

Many people are unable to separate the stereotyped person from the actual person. The prevalence of implicit bias has been well documented since the 1998 release of Harvard University's Implicit Association Test (IAT). In an analysis of IAT results, researchers at the Perception Institute note, "A significant majority of Whites as well as Asian Americans and Latinos show anti-Black bias in the IAT and almost half of African Americans also show anti-Black bias" (Johnson & Godsil, 2013, p. 8). When the single most significant image of contemporary Latino and Hispanic people in the United States is that of the undocumented, "illegal," and "alien," imagine the challenge Spanish-speaking children and their parents face in their efforts to authentically "be." Consider the fear that some Arab American and Muslim children must feel when their narrative includes "being terrorists."

In many ways, teachers are taught to believe that what they have to teach children will, in the end, save them. In a perfect world, this might well be true. But while children of color may not be able to identify the burdens they carry, I believe they are intensely aware of the consequences those burdens have on their lives. They might believe that there is really no point to school or that it is somehow a betrayal to their family and friends to surrender themselves to the education process. Some of our children feel a level of mistrust of teachers and administrators at a very early age (Rhoden, 2017). Many children feel that their behavior is inconsequential and unrelated to their education. These are just a few signs that manifest the heavy weight our children bear each day.

From kindergarten, these children are already trying to scale a mountain they are unprepared to climb, as unprepared as their guides (the teachers) are to help them. Imagine being lost at the beginning of a long journey, and the one person who steps forward to help is someone you can't trust. You don't know why you can't trust them; you just can't. The energy that drives this distrust is guilt. Many children are blocked from trusting by the burden of guilt they carry with them. And much of our behavior as teachers unintentionally validates their feelings. To go back to the guide metaphor, suppose *you* are the appointed guide, and after a year or two of trying to help, you've come to the conclusion that no matter how hard you try, you won't be able to get that person up the mountain. Even if children manage to overcome their challenges and excel as students, they will always feel that weight. It will affect their choices and experiences throughout their lives.

The guilt propagated by stereotyping has a ripple effect in school, widening the achievement gap and hindering the growth of positive relationships. These elements are interconnected, but in the following sections I discuss each aspect in turn to elucidate how it comes about and how it hurts our children.

The Achievement Gap

Advances in the study of cognition (Kang, 2005) have firmly established that the subconscious mind is working overtime to contextualize our experiences. Stereotypes work extremely well at the subconscious level. They literally rest there. Set down roots there. Our children are taught by the whispers of the world around them what to be. The idea that they are constantly making choices about right and wrong is, I believe, a specious one. They are taught how to think. What to value. Who to be.

Who is doing this? Who creates the images, the stories about us that take root in our cultural landscape? The racial history of America is a part of that landscape—a part of the land and the scape (DeGruy, 2005). We have a way of measuring the lasting impact of radioactivity in Chernobyl, but not of our recovery from slavery. Obviously, racism has a half-life.

This thing called *race,* that people created and defined, that is very real and yet made up, stands in all of our way. Our society is still mired in its tendrils.

We don't like to admit it. In fact, we do as much as we can to convince ourselves of the opposite. This has something to do with an American desire to "achieve" innocence with regard to race. I used the word *achieve* to denote that the United States has never experienced innocence when it comes to race. When it applies to race, the facts speak through the American consciousness in a stream that cannot escape the guilt that history demands. America is not so much trying to *regain* a lost innocence as it is struggling to *achieve* it.

However we think about race, we use it in many ways. One of its most damaging functions is the way it is used against children— for example, to lower our expectations of children of color or even dehumanize them (Epstein, Blake, & González, 2017; Gilliam, Maupin, Reyes, Accavitti, & Shic, 2016; Goff, Jackson, Di Leone, Culotta, & DiTomasso, 2014). And, to the point of this book, we use race to calculate the damage that an ineffective education system does to children, commonly expressed as an "achievement gap." Disparities are the language of race: what *you* get is different from what *they* get.

For example, in Boston, white children perform significantly better than black children, with "24% of black and 26% of Hispanic students in grades 3 through 8" scoring "above grade-level proficiency in MCAS reading last year, compared to 63% of white and 62% of Asian students" (Sobey, 2019, para. 2). Likewise, in Seattle, white children perform roughly 40 percent better than black children in math and English language arts (Bazzaz, 2018). In fact, "Of the 100 major U.S. cities, eight have small achievement gaps, 25 have large achievement gaps and 67 have massive achievement gaps" (Education Cities, 2016, p. 15). National statistics document decades of disparities in academic performance between white and black children and white and Hispanic children on reading and math assessments (Musu-Gillette et al., 2017).

Simply put, black children fail at a greater rate than white children. That's what the numbers say. You know—the numbers that come from the standardized tests that students are required to take, which are conceptualized and prepared in the same environment that already has accounted for their failure.

We can further deduce from these reports that black and brown children will have greater disciplinary problems, experience higher unemployment, be subject to more criminalization and incarceration, be poorer, have lower rates of college education, and so on. This is the toll our system of education takes on our children. And teachers are witnesses to this tragedy.

The Relationship Gap

Every year, when the failure of the public education system is announced, there is much agonizing. But somehow, each year, the agony sounds less and less genuine. Each year, the debates and discussions about how to address the problem of the achievement gap seem less urgent and passionate. Research abounds on the depth of the problem, while ideas and projects to address the problem—usually in the form of diversity training or cultural proficiency training—proliferate. Yet the problem persists. As a nation, we watch as our beautiful, creative children are marginalized further by the education system. It is as if we are slowly being conditioned to accept this failure. It sometimes seems that there is no viable way to solve what appears to be an intractable situation.

African American children (boys and girls) continue to be punished for being black. Latino and Hispanic students suffer for being Latino and Hispanic. Indigenous children suffer for being born who they are. Arab American and Muslim children are locked into the stereotypes created by a system that needs a way to characterize them. To cite just one egregious example of this sad state of affairs, in 2015, 14-year-old Ahmed Mohamed built a homemade alarm clock and brought it to school to present to his teacher. He was detained by police and suspended from school after "educators accused him of building a fake bomb. The White House press secretary stated: 'This episode is a good illustration of how pernicious stereotypes can prevent even good-hearted people who have dedicated their lives to educating young people from doing the good work that they set out to do'" (Fernandez & Hauser, 2015). These children become numbers in a landslide of statistics documenting the damage of stereotypes.

When our children enter their classrooms each year, the reality that awaits them is one of low expectations, disconnection, and academic cynicism. And let's be clear: although family looms large, it is not the problem. Curriculum is not the problem. School administrators are not precisely the problem. And finally, no, the teachers are not the problem, either.

Quite simply, in my opinion, the problem has to do with our children's inability to believe that anyone really sees or cares about them (Yeager, Purdie-Vaughns, Hooper, & Cohen, 2017). Therein lies our challenge: to make educators relevant to children from a child's point of view. To disrupt the provisional reality that our culture has constructed for our children and ourselves. To make the role of education and educators in our children's lives essential and felt. Children must be reconnected to the adults who are charged with educating them.

The so-called achievement gap is inextricably linked to a relationship gap: as Hattie (2009) found, "It is teachers. . . who have created positive student-teacher relationships that are more likely to have the above average effects on student achievement" (p. 126). If the entire system made a commitment to engage each student as a specific child with specific needs and to connect each child with their teacher; if every teacher were prepared and excited to get to know each child; if every educator were challenged, as a part of their job, to *know* the children they are expected to teach, then those students would perform completely differently than their history might indicate.

I know this because this is exactly the work I've been doing for more than eight years now.

The popular images of black, Hispanic or Latino, or Indigenous children never include the scholar; the stereotypes are almost all negative. So why should we expect our children to behave differently in the classroom? Many of them have never actually had the opportunity to live as children. Our children hardly get a chance to simply *be*.

But what if educators, beginning in preschool, were able to help liberate our children from the chains of these stereotypes? What would happen?

Constructing the Innocent Classroom

There is an answer to the serious and life-limiting, even life-threatening, problems confronting U.S. public education. If guilt is the primary barrier for children of color in the classroom, then the solution is to restore and maintain their innocence. In fact, it is my contention that teaching innocence is one of the most important things a teacher can do.

Let us begin with a common understanding of innocence as it is discussed in this book:

Innocence is the condition that results from the reduction, minimization, neutralization, or elimination of the guilt that develops from stereotypes and popular negative narratives and iconography.

The driving force of my insistence on innocence in the classroom for all students, but especially for students of color, derives from the assertion that innocence is an essential and fundamental human quality that it is important for *all* of us to consciously experience and understand. Many children of color don't know what it feels like to walk America's streets and feel safe and innocent—and unless we intervene, most of them never will know. In its 2019 analysis of the NYPD's stop-and-frisk data, the New York Civil Liberties Union reports that "black and Latino people were disproportionately stopped regardless of the demographic make-up of the neighborhood. For example, in the 17th precinct, which encompasses Kips Bay and Murray Hill, black and Latino people make up just 8 percent of the population but 75 percent of the people stopped by police" (para. 7).

Innocence is an immeasurably beautiful and important gift that all teachers can give their students. When children believe that what they are being taught can have a positive impact on their lives and that they deserve the lessons they are being taught, and when they can walk the halls of a school or enter a classroom without the weight of negative expectations, they will respond more positively to the academic challenges put before them.

The Innocent Classroom, described throughout the course of this book, is a professional development experience I launched in 2012 to change how teachers think about and engage students of color. The approach articulates a nationwide need to reform teacher-student interaction in a way that can dramatically reduce, if not eradicate, disparities for all marginalized children and free them to achieve. To accomplish this end, the Innocent Classroom does something no other response to disparity does: it offers a process for creating relationships. Essentially, the Innocent Classroom is a practical methodology for building active and functional relationships with each child in your classroom.

The Innocent Classroom is a place where children are allowed to exist without the weight of the negative stereotypes, iconography, and narratives that so profoundly affect their lives. Outside the classroom, to some, they may be just another representation of some stereotype. But inside your classroom, none of that touches them.

How do you create this environment? How do you build a relationship with a child that opens them to believing that you see them this way? This is what we are going to tackle in this book: how relationships can be constructed between a teacher and a child in such a way that the child will, at least temporarily, be a willing and engaged student under your tutelage.

PRACTICE

The Innocent Classroom is a continual practice, not a project that is complete after finishing this book. It is a way of approaching a diverse classroom, especially one with children of color in it. Each time you are given a new class, at the beginning of the year or semester, the process is repeated. To begin your practice, think about your answer to the following question.

Whom do you admire most?

The Goals of the Innocent Classroom

A fundamental goal of the Innocent Classroom is for all teachers, staff, and administrators to embrace the idea that innocence is an absolute necessity for each child. The knowledge of innocence, a clear belief in it within and for themselves, is an essential element in children's academic, social, and emotional growth. We want to increase students' capacity to learn effectively and to understand how their learning will actually change their lives. We want to reveal to our students that much of what society projects as a representation of who they are are fabrications that are incomplete or flat-out wrong. We want to help our students see their place in the world.

Most of all, we want to relieve our children of the weight of guilt, because we know those inaccurate perceptions undermine their capacity to believe in the efficacy of their education.

PRACTICE

Take a moment to write the answer to this question.

What don't you have that you wish you did?

Now think about one of your students. How would they answer? Find the time soon to actually ask that student.

The Teacher's Role

The Innocent Classroom frees children from their bondage to stereotypes by turning educators into liberators. Teachers can become the transformational force that makes innocence possible for the children they are charged with educating. But to take on this role, educators must commit to developing authentic, intentional relationships with all students, creating classrooms where children are free of negative expectations. The following scenario, which asks you to put yourself in the shoes of a student, illustrates the power teachers have to hand children their innocence.

Seeing Innocence

Imagine you are a 10-year-old African American boy sitting in a 4th grade classroom. The noise of your house, the life you left behind earlier this morning, and the events of the previous evening all recede, and you now find yourself in an environment that is wholly unlike home. Still, it is a place that you are familiar with. You've been coming to this place for several years now, and it has become a regular thing. You have become relatively comfortable with the controlled chaos that surrounds you and that in many ways defines this place called school.

At this point in your school life, you've made some decisions. You've committed yourself to being quiet, or, if you've found you can't be quiet, you've decided to be vocal. You've chosen to have a lot of friends, only a few, or hardly any at all. You've chosen to care about what you look like to others, or you've chosen not to care. You've made a lot of choices, actually.

Maybe you are a carefree child who is loved by your parents, or maybe your life doesn't allow for "carefree," and you often surrender to a darker, brooding demeanor. Maybe you generally feel happy, or maybe happiness is so rare that you don't really know what it is.

But you sit at your desk and respond as well as you can to the teacher who stands at the front of the classroom. You may try to do the work that is expected of you, or you may not. Maybe you've already decided that the teacher doesn't like you or asks too much of you or doesn't care whether you do it or not. Maybe *you* don't care.

Maybe you like being in this room, at this desk, for five or six hours every day, because it allows you to escape everywhere else. It may be better in here than out there. Of course, whenever someone asks you if you would rather be out there, you always say yes, you hate school. Maybe you actually don't, but you've already learned that most kids your age say that they hate school. What else would someone expect you to say?

You do like the time you get to play in a relatively safe place like the schoolyard or the gym. You like that there's food to eat. And you like some of the grownups you've met here, even though the way they interact with you is different than it is out there.

School sometimes seems irrelevant. Except that you realize, as you struggle to read the books you're supposed to read, that learning to read has its advantages. Everyone has to learn how to read, but not many people out there endorse the functional value of reading, or of school for that matter. Maybe there aren't a lot of books in your house. Maybe no one is ever curled up on the couch with a book in their hands.

But you can read, and sometimes you actually find it enjoyable. There are stories you like. It helps being able to understand things better. You can see how much you've changed and grown since kindergarten. But it's getting harder and harder. There are more and more kids who seem to care less and less about the work they're supposed to be doing.

You're learning how social everything is. Everyone sees you in a certain way. You realized that last year, when your allergies were acting up and your nose was running all the time and the fluids dried in streams on your face, that kids and even some adults would avoid looking at you. You learned to carry tissues. You learned that when your shoes started falling apart, somebody had to buy you new ones. They had to. You knew kids that never got new shoes. You didn't want to be one of them.

But there were days when nothing made sense. Days when you were tired and crabby and this woman was standing there staring at you asking for something you forgot to do or chose not to do, knowing that this moment would come but being willing to risk it. Days like today.

You are angry. You're not really sure why. You could probably offer a list of things that are bothering you to someone who cared. But really . . . really, you're just angry. And this woman is staring at you, and it makes everything worse.

Get off my case, lady.

Get the f— off my case.

I don't care what you're talking about.

I don't care about you.

Her stare hardens. Now she's angry. You know that look. You've gotten that look from her before, been in this situation before. You've cursed at her before, called her a bitch, even. But you don't care about her. You don't care that she's angry. What's she got to be angry about? She's the one standing over you, putting pressure on you. Who wants to deal with this B.S. on a day like today?

But today, she's doing something different. You expected a pass to the vice principal. An invitation to go somewhere and cool off. To the office or somewhere where there was someone waiting to calm you down. Been there, done that.

But today she's coming toward you. This white lady who is your teacher. She's coming toward you, and you're waiting to see exactly how she will receive your anger. She bends down and says in a voice that only you can hear, "Adam. This is where I usually send you to the office. But I'm not doing that today. And I'm not putting you in time-out. I've been watching you. Paying really special attention to you. And you know what?"

You are a little surprised at this approach, not sure what is coming. But you can't stop your brain from asking, "What?" You don't say it, but you're thinking it.

"I've noticed that you're always drawing airplanes. They are everywhere on your papers."

OK, so you like airplanes. So what?

"Did I ever tell you that my brother flies airplanes for an airline? Maybe I could get you some models. Would you like that?"

You nod your head slowly, reflexively.

She stands up straight and looks you in the eye. And in her eyes, you can see something you've never seen before, something inchoate. You can't quite name it yet. Maybe it's warmth. Or a commitment to try to see something in you. Maybe it's a recognition that there is, in fact, something to see. Yes. That's it.

She smiles. "We'll talk about it later," she says.

And that was it.

All you did was nod your head.

We must acknowledge that despite everything we have absorbed from popular culture and pernicious racial stereotypes, all the children who sit before us are innocent or have the capacity to reacquire what innocence they have lost. We must teach the value of innocence and create an environment where innocence is expected. And we must understand that innocence—allowing a child to feel free, for at least six hours, of the suspicious, tainted eye of society—is a significant precondition to children's capacity to learn (Yeager et al., 2014).

Unfortunately, restoring, nurturing, and advocating for the innocence and consequent goodness of students is the one set of skills in which teachers have the least training (Civic Enterprises, Bridgeland, Bruce, & Hariharan, 2013). Our schools of education have not provided the right kind of training to teachers for the times we live in and for the children they are charged with teaching. An experiential and theoretical understanding of innocence and a belief in possibility is necessary to fully understand their potential. The natural outcome of innocence in the classroom is a child's growing belief in the possibility of success.

To play their part in the Innocent Classroom, teachers must first understand three things:

1. Race is a social construct and therefore not an explanation for academic success or failure. We—meaning people—created race in a way that works for some and injures others (Haney-López, 1996).
2. The subconscious mind—where stereotypes take root—is more powerful than we are often willing to admit (Greenwald, McGhee, & Schwartz, 1998).
3. The knowledge of one's own innocence is fundamental to one's capacity to grow. I believe that the memory of innocence, the experience of it in our lives, is an important element in our ability to see its absence and the guilt that is the residue of negatively stereotyping the children we are charged with educating.

If these three ideas can be internalized, the restoration and protection of children's innocence is also possible.

The Power of the Innocent Classroom

The Innocent Classroom has the potential to transform classroom culture and outcomes. In an Innocent Classroom, students' behavior and academic engagement improve. Their belief in the system grows.

Teachers have testified to these results. After completing Innocent Classroom training,

- Ninety-two percent of educators reported an increase in academic mindset when they used Innocent Classroom strategies to engage a child.
- Eighty-seven percent of educators reported seeing greater-than-usual academic growth in some or most of their students as a result of their participation in Innocent Classroom training.
- Eighty-six percent of educators reported stronger relationships with students as a result of Innocent Classroom training.
- Eighty-eight percent of educators reported being better able to positively redirect student behavior because of their Innocent Classroom training.
- Educators reported a 40 percent reduction in weekly disciplinary referrals since beginning participation in Innocent Classroom training. (Innocent Technologies, 2018)

Directly following our first session, the impact that the discussions, shared experiences, and philosophy of the Innocent Classroom had on me was quite profound. The experience served as a reminder of what I had already felt to be true: all children are inherently good. The place where our students are when they come to us need not be the place where we start with them. We, as thinking, creative, and caring educators, have the ability to help rewrite their story—to create a new starting point, as it were.

The Innocent Classroom helps me focus on the reason I originally chose education as a career: to nurture the well-being of children. Knowing that other educators think and feel in similar ways makes my journey stronger and more purposeful.

—*Elementary reading facilitator, Omaha, NE*

It's important to keep in mind the intended scope of this approach and to set expectations accordingly. This is the Innocent *Classroom,* which is to say that the changes you see in your students will be limited, at least initially, to your classroom or area within the school. When beginning the effort to create an Innocent Classroom, it is crucial to keep your focus on the behavior and academic engagement of each student in your classroom. A student's relationship with another teacher or behavior in another class is not your immediate priority. You cannot expect that the change you see in your classroom will have a life outside your room. The change you see will stem from the change in *your* relationship with the student. Later, when that relationship has matured a bit, you may be able to influence that child's performance outside your classroom.

How to Read This Book

In Innocent Classroom training sessions, participants engage in discussions about much of what you've just read in this Introduction. Educators from preK through 12th grade, in a diverse array of roles—including bus drivers, cafeteria workers, counselors, disciplinary staff, and administrators—have participated in Innocent Classroom trainings. These sessions present a particular way of looking at the contemporary challenges that face marginalized children, especially children of color, in the U.S. education system. However, I've written this book for the individual educator. Although groups of educators have the benefit of collegial support and critique, even individual educators who engage in this effort have seen significant transformations in the quality of relationships with their students. But it also makes sense that as groups of educators near you begin to consider the Innocent Classroom, you might form book study groups to discuss the practices outlined herein.

I understand that awareness about the cultural, racial, sexual, and gender histories and realities that most educators are engaged in underpin our journey of constructing the Innocent Classroom, and context is important. We all come to this work at different stages of understanding the complexity of contemporary American culture. A successful educator of the Innocent Classroom will also be engaged in the process of understanding the general consequences and implications of these concerns. The important thing in the training of Innocent Classroom educators is that the main focus be on increasing the quality of student-teacher relationships within the classroom. Everything else, including issues that exist outside the classroom, is secondary.

The Process in Brief: The Six Stages of Progression to the Innocent Classroom

I look at the Innocent Classroom as, above all, a project of constructing relationships. With that in mind, let's look at the six stages of this construction project, divided by chapter.

In Chapter 1, we deepen our understanding of the dilemma that children of color face with respect to guilt and innocence, explore the ways in which the weight of guilt is bestowed on them, examine what the research says about stereotype consciousness and stereotype threat, and explore how to start building a new educational operating system.

In Chapter 2, we explore the ways educators can begin to recognize and measure the innocence deficit of each child and then to strategize ways of creating an authentic relationship with that child. We focus on being able to recognize the good in children of color and to see the way each child responds to the weight of guilt they've been saddled with.

In Chapter 3, we talk about valuing, on multiple levels. We want to value the progress we've made, value the time we have with students, value students' innocence, and model for students the belief that innocence is a valuable aspect of their personality and their behavior in the classroom. This important stage will increase our capacity to identify and respond to students' good.

Chapter 4 offers prompts and Innocent Classroom "laboratory" examples to walk you through the process of engaging and developing strategic responses to students' good.

Chapter 5 shares strategies for nurturing students' innocence and managing and maintaining the fledgling Innocent Classroom.

Chapter 6 discusses the final phase of our construction project, where we actively guard and help children guard their reclaimed innocence and understanding of their own good. The classroom will have been converted into a space where students can leave guilt at the door, no longer feel the threat of negative stereotypes, and are free to express their curiosity for learning.

These are the goals we set to transform our children's learning experience. These stages capture the essence of the Constructing the Innocent Classroom training that we at Innocent Technologies have shared with thousands of educators during the last eight years. After all, my desire to infuse our current education system with the concepts and approaches of the Innocent Classroom won't bear fruit unless there is a wide-ranging discussion of its merits and application of its principles, which I hope this work will stimulate.

1 Deepening Understanding

Let's begin our construction project by outlining an overarching, two-pronged objective. First, we want to create an enhanced classroom environment for marginalized children that will positively affect their social and academic outcomes. Note the presence of "academic" alongside "social." Although the principal focus of the Innocent Classroom is building teacher-student relationships, the ultimate goal of this work is to address the achievement gap—to place our children in an environment where they are free to achieve academic success. We must continuously remind ourselves of this, because all too often, nurturing positive social-emotional development comes at the cost of academic achievement. It's crucial to academically challenge students *while* strengthening relationships with them.

The second part of our objective is to know our students well enough to construct the class environment in such a way that it encourages the fullest engagement from the most wounded. To get here, educators must take a circuitous route that requires them to examine the origin and implications of the guilt students bear and to gather knowledge about who each child is. Constructing the Innocent Classroom begins with a recognition that the relationship you develop with each child is the key indicator in your capacity to help them let go of the script that holds them back. It is your knowledge of each child's life that will open the door to that relationship.

Accordingly, in this chapter, we will deepen our understanding of the dilemma that children of color face with respect to guilt and innocence by looking at the ways in which the weight of guilt is bestowed on them. We will examine what the research says about stereotype consciousness and stereotype threat. Finally, we will explore how to start building a new educational operating system—chiefly, by gathering knowledge about our children and understanding that they all have their own "good."

> Every single child deserves to believe that school is for them and that their educators care about them. Every single child deserves to believe that the world is open to them and their growth. Building an authentic relationship with a child based on their humanity shows them that they deserve to be a part of our society and that it is possible to meet every standard. Innocence for a child of color is a belief that they can be deeply and authentically loved by their educators. Innocence is entering a space and always assuming it is possible to be loved. When a child of color has a sense of their own innocence, they believe that they can be loved for who they truly are.
>
> —*Innocent Classroom trainer*

The List

Defining and reclaiming innocence in the lives of our children requires us to first discuss its opposite: guilt. Guilt is more easily identified, more familiar to us, than innocence. In an environment that presumes and enables guilt, its presence is written into our thoughts and our language.

Years ago, I taught a college class on contemporary African American male novelists. The first time I taught this course, I stood at the board and asked my students to shout out one-word descriptions of black men. I was curious to hear their preconceived thoughts about the male protagonists of the texts we would be reading. After a moment of hesitation, the words came at me like a shower of spitballs. *Threatening. Violent. Fast. Strong. Angry. Athletic. Rhythmic. Rageful. Irresponsible. Sexy. Loud. Dancers. Singers. Drunks. Criminal. Sneaky. Big. Lazy.*

By the time they were done, I was exhausted and, I must admit, sad. There were very few words that were wholly positive; even the seemingly positive ones *felt* negative within the context of the list. On the one hand, I was pleased that my students felt comfortable enough with me to be so open and honest. On the other hand, I was shocked at how solidly negative their impressions had been. And later that night, as I thought about it, I got angry.

Why didn't my students know about my father, or any of the other men in my family? Why didn't they know about my neighborhood, or my friends who personified the responsible, ethical, beautiful, intellectual, resourceful, honest, law-abiding, and diplomatic qualities that I have come to see and expect in many African American men? And heaven knows, the one word I longed to have attached to my existence—*safe*—has perhaps never been used in a sentence about a black man.

At the next class, I put my list before the class. We shared a profound experience. Most of the students were white, and most of them couldn't remember when their attitudes about black men had soured. But they all had a clear memory of a time in their lives when they were free of such poison. When they could see goodness in the faces of anonymous black men.

Almost all of them felt that the cumulative exposure to the fears of their parents and popular media—news, movies, music, and so on— had something to do with the change in their fundamental feelings about black men in America. They were taught to fear me, to mistrust me. Our culture broadcasts abbreviated and coded realities of black humanity that make compassion and understanding hard to come by.

Over the years, I've seen many similar responses to that exercise. One especially hit me hard. A young pregnant black woman wrote in her class journal that the discussion forced her to admit her anger and mistrust of African American men. She talked about the baby boy that she carried in her belly and how much work she had to do to be ready for him. Him, a young black boy.

This pollution seeps deep into the fabric of our society.

My student's unborn son and all of us who began life as black boys share this awful legacy. No matter what we have done, no matter how hard we have worked or how long we have served, we are unfortunately privileged to know that people think these things about us.

My students provided me with a list of stereotypes associated with being African American, but other groups of people of color get their own lists, of course. My experience bears out that when you gather any group of people, including teachers, and ask them to be honest about what they've been told about Latinos, Indigenous peoples, Asian Americans, or African Americans, there is a list at the ready. The qualities and characteristics on these lists absolutely indict our society as one that consistently—though not always consciously—demonizes people of color (Greenwald, Poehlman, Uhlmann, & Banaji, 2009). And while all this is happening to adults, our children are absorbing it at alarming rates.

What Does American Culture Tell You About the Children You Teach?

We must fully acknowledge the breadth of the stereotypes that have been promulgated about people of color. How virulent they are. How deeply each of us has been affected by the cumulative weight of negative narratives about people of color.

Now take a deep breath and make your own list. What does American culture tell you about the children you teach or are responsible for?

When I started writing this book, I planned to include a list from one of our Innocent Classroom training sessions, created by the educators we work with, but I eventually decided not to. Your list will suffice, and it will mean more to you. Just make sure to be honest in this exercise. Your personal beliefs about race and culture are immaterial; what matters is your ability to decode and acknowledge the way our culture has created stories and images about people.

What does American culture tell you about children of color? What does our society tell you about the children you teach? Record your list in the space below.

The Cumulative Impact of Negative Stereotypes

Living with stereotypes is a limiting, destructive, and psychologically debilitating way to go through life. In the Innocent Classroom, guilt is defined as *the cumulative impact of negative stereotypes that affect attitude and behavior; the absence of innocence.*

Guilt becomes a barrier in the development of relationships between teachers and students. The list you made above has already been made by the children in your classroom. They've committed it to memory. In many ways, for many children of color, this list might be seen as the origin of their disidentification with academic achievement. If we know that these negative stereotypes about them exist, our children know it, too. Some of our children may already believe that this is their destiny. Guilt provides them with a script for where they are and where they're going.

Again, I want you to assume that your list exists within the consciousness of many of the children of color in your class. You should also accept that many of them already believe that *you* believe all the stereotypes about them. These stereotypes weigh on our children as if they were already lived experiences and are converted, emotionally, into actual guilt. This guilt imbues children with a sense that they have done something wrong before they've actually done it. It's no surprise, then, that guilt triggers cynicism, anger, apathy, and a general sense of opposition to education. Our children get the sense that it doesn't really matter what they do or how they behave; the world will see them as guilty because that is the way the world sees them already. Unfortunately, most of our children exhibit the negative consequences of this guilt before they even know what motivates their behavior. According to McKown and Weinstein (2003),

> Between ages 6 and 10, children's ability to infer an individual's stereotype increases dramatically. Children's awareness of broadly held stereotypes also increases with age, and children from academically stigmatized ethnic groups (African Americans and Latinos) are at all ages more likely be aware of broadly held stereotypes than children from academically nonstigmatized ethnic groups (Whites and Asians). (p. 498)

This is the dilemma of children of color. They know that they are problems or problems-to-be. I can't help thinking of W. E. B. Du Bois's classic *The Souls of Black Folk* (1903), in which he asks, "How does it feel to be a problem?" (p. 1).

In the absence of innocence, guilt thrives and accumulates over time. From the moment a child is followed by the keen, suspicious eye of a department store detective or disrespectfully challenged by a police officer, from the first moment they can detect from anyone in a position of authority a sign of double standards, negative expectations, or malicious patronization, the weight of guilt begins to accumulate. Any indication that they are the subject of stereotyping and marginalization simply adds to this weight. Part of their job, as children of color, is to learn how to manage this weight and survive. Their immediate goal may not necessarily be to perform well in school, but simply to endure the rattling weight of guilt that they are quickly gathering within themselves.

The Research on Stereotype Consciousness and Stereotype Threat

As I developed the Innocent Classroom training process, I came across the work of researchers who analyze the impact of stereotypes on students of color. Their research makes it clear that children are deeply affected by a "consciousness" about stereotypes that resides within them (McKown & Weinstein, 2003). McKown and Strambler (2009) define this *stereotype consciousness* as "knowledge that others endorse beliefs about the characteristics of ethnic groups" (p. 1643).

The danger of stereotype consciousness is that it can easily trigger *stereotype threat*—"the fear that one's behavior may confirm or be understood in terms of a negative stereotype associated with one's social group" (Guyll, Madon, Prieto, & Scherr, 2010). Stereotype threat has been shown in multiple studies to lower performance of a target group on achievement tests. In multiple tests, and with multiple "outgroups" (blacks, women, immigrants, and so on), targets' performance has flagged when their knowledge of mainstream stereotypes of their group have been "primed" (Guyll et al., 2010; McKown & Strambler, 2009; Spencer, Steele, & Quinn, 1999). As Spencer and colleagues' groundbreaking 1999 study showed, "stereotype threat decreases performance on tasks that are associated with a stereotype-relevant domain because it generates a disruptive pressure akin to anxiety" (Guyll et al., 2010, p. 120).

Summarizing his work with Claude Steele, Joshua Aronson (2004) explicates how stereotype threat can hamper achievement:

> I've come to believe that human intellectual performance is far more fragile than we customarily think; it can rise and fall depending on the social context. As research is showing, conditions that threaten basic motives—such as our sense of competence, our feelings of belonging, and our trust in people around us—can dramatically influence our intellectual capacities and how stereotypes suppress the performance, motivation, and learning of students who have to contend with them. (para. 14)

Unfortunately, the ramifications of stereotype threat do not end with academic performance. As Guyll and colleagues (2010) explain, the phenomenon may have a cascading effect:

> Stereotype threat can lower performance, and such direct effects could produce additional consequences. First, teachers may falsely believe that poor performance reflects true ability, thereby setting a self-fulfilling prophecy in motion. Second, stereotype threat's negative effects on test scores could reduce a student's chances of gaining admission to a quality school. Third, a student who must repeatedly contend with stereotype threat may, over time, disidentify with academics. Disidentification serves to distance one's identity from the threatening domain and, by so doing, strips away the desire and motivation to excel. Disidentification can influence student choices that fundamentally alter their education and career trajectories (Steele, 1997). (p. 121)

Lisa Delpit (2012) endorses this conclusion, noting that "black students today, as perhaps never before, are victims of the myths of inferiority and find much less support for countering these myths and embracing academic achievement outside of individual families than at other times in the past" (p. 42). In their book *Generations of Exclusion: Mexican Americans, Assimilation, and Race,* Edward Telles and Vilma Ortiz (2008) warn of similar effects that propagating racist stereotypes will engender now and far into the future:

> The signals and racial stereotypes that educators and society send to students affect the extent to which they will engage and persist in school. Racial stereotypes produce a positive self-identity for white and Asian students but a negative one for blacks and Latinos, which affect school success. . . . Racialized self-perceptions among Mexican American students generally endure into the third and fourth generations. (p. 132)

Mary J. Fischer's (2010) study on outcomes for students of color at elite institutions showed that black and Latino students who had internalized stereotypes about their group "were found to spend fewer hours studying than those who reported less negative stereotypes about their own group" (p. 22).

If we are to be honest, we must accept that stereotypes are pervasive in our culture. We must also accept that teachers are not immune to them. No matter how hard we work to prepare ourselves to teach a diverse population of students, chances are, we hold negative stereotypes within our conscious and unconscious minds. As Christine Reyna (2000) writes,

> Stereotypes pervade educational and achievement domains, from the classroom to the playground, from the dean's office to the advisor's office, from the time a child enters preschool until they retire. Stereotypes can impede people's goals through catalyzing and justifying negative evaluations and punitive or rejecting behaviors toward the stereotyped. Stereotypes also create internal barriers to success by propagating self-doubt, dashed hopes for the future, or lost confidence in an environment that does not let the stereotyped succeed. And although they are too numerous to count, the multitude of possible stereotypes have very specific consequences for the way students are judged and treated by their teachers and peers, and for the way students perceive their own capabilities and potentials. (p. 106)

The research is clear that teachers' perceptions of students can directly affect student performance and evaluation. Gary L. St. C. Oates (2003) states,

> Teacher perceptions . . . may facilitate perpetuation of the black-white gap even if they arise from a process that is largely race neutral. Jussim, Eccles, and Madon (1996) observe an intriguing tendency for teachers' subjective assessments to exert stronger effects on subsequent grades and standardized mathematics test scores of African-American (vis-à-vis white) students. Thus, unfavorable teacher perceptions, even if justified by prior performance and other relevant information, may more strongly undermine the performance of African-American students. (p. 509)

Renee White-Clark (2005) adds, "Research indicates that how teachers relate to students in terms of attitudes and perceptions is one of the critical factors in how students learn. Teacher misconceptions can lead to minority students being misunderstood, miseducated, and possibly mistreated" (p. 25). This is especially problematic given the fact that students from culturally, economically, and racially marginalized groups often need high teacher expectations as well as rigorous and creative instructional practices to succeed in school (Silver, Smith, & Nelson, 1995; Sorhagen, 2013). Sadly, these are not being provided. Studies have shown that, on average, black and Latino students are given less attention and receive more negative feedback and mixed messages than their white peers (Irvine, 1986; Rubovits & Maehr, 1973).

A growing body of literature also focuses on the fact that subtle messages of disdain, such as those communicated through stereotypes, can be even more harmful to students than outright racism, as Maximino Plata (2011) notes:

> [C]overt ethnocentric behaviors aimed at culturally, linguistically, and economically diverse students may be more dangerous than overt ethnocentric behaviors because covert behaviors cannot be seen, heard or touched. Therefore, these students cannot defend against what they cannot see, hear or touch. In any case, expressions of ethnocentricism usually have dire consequences for all individuals, but the consequences seem to be more profound for individuals from suppressed cultural groups. (p. 118)

Indeed, the "veiled" ethnocentrism of stereotypes, Plata (2011) argues, can end up working in a kind of feedback loop, with teacher stereotypes fueling student behavior and teacher perceptions of student behavior, which then provide more "evidence" for the pervasive stereotype. He writes,

> The cumulative effect of teachers' instructional and managerial decisions based on their culturally laden cognitive schemata has historically served to deepen negative stereotypes about culturally, linguistically, and economically diverse students. Students who possess cultural and language attributes that differ from those of their teachers become lightning rods for teachers' instructional and

disciplinary practices. Furthermore, these students' cultural and language differences conveniently serve as reasons or explanations for their low academic achievement, lack of motivation, lags in reading and math achievement, lack of acculturation, speech problems, etc. (pp. 118–119)

According to Delpit (2012), stunted student growth and limited social and academic engagement are the inevitable result of subconscious endorsement of negative student stereotypes. She writes, "What happens when we assume that certain children are less than brilliant? Our tendency is to teach less, to teach down, to teach for remediation. Without having any intention of discriminating, we can do harm to children who are viewed within a stereotype of 'less than'" (p. 6).

The research makes it clear: we must actively work to diminish the influence of negative stereotypes on our relationships with marginalized children. This is precisely the work of the Innocent Classroom.

A New Operating System

Think about the work of constructing the Innocent Classroom as a manual reformatting of the traditional classroom's operating system. The traditional classroom has its benefits, but fostering relationships with disaffected or disconnected children is not one of them. Even when they focus on building relationships, traditional programs often fall short and may do more harm than good. For example, one such program

trained teachers to form instrumental relationships with students, connecting with them through the use of discrete moves, in a unidirectional fashion, purely as a means of improving their behavior and effort on teacher directed tasks. . . . The graduates from [this] program went on to serve students of color from low-income backgrounds. . . . The instrumental relationships imposed upon the students of color from low-income backgrounds were structured as a controlled means to a particular end: student compliance. Teachers took in just enough information about students to use in class to motivate them to keep

working and behaving, while providing discrete positive reinforce-
ment and punishment to ensure no one strayed. Students learned
that their value was tied to the degree to which they worked hard and
behaved in line with what mostly white authority figures demanded,
not in their own right. (Theisen-Homer, 2018, paras. 2, 3)

By contrast, the Innocent Classroom provides an intentional way
of approaching a diverse classroom, especially one with children of
color in it, that is also child-specific: each child has their own configuration of guilt and their own innocence deficit. Each child has
their own *good*—that is, motivation behind their behavior (more on
this in Chapter 2). This foundational understanding is a paradigm
shift from the old teacher-centered system. The Innocent Classroom
is an operating system built for the times we live in, to minimize the
individual stresses and traumas of marginalized children. Like any
effective operating system, it operates in the background. But unlike
a computer-based operating system, it cannot be instantly booted up;
you have to build it.

To do so, you need to understand the specificities of the guilt your
students carry and help them jettison it. You need to acknowledge
their innocence and discern their good by carefully observing them,
asking them questions, and challenging them. This is not about judg-
ing students' academic potential or weighing the veracity of your
notions about their behavior, good or bad. Rather, this is about engaging with them simply to know them better and validate their good,
eventually accumulating enough knowledge to establish authentic
relationships with them. It is a subtle but disarming process; students
will become conscious that you are curious about them in the most
meaningful of ways. This sparked connection is the path to helping
students reevaluate the significance of innocence in their life, influ-
encing the development of their good over time, and challenging them
to make their good present in their real world.

I know that many teachers already do this. It is a natural consequence of having compassionate hearts and caring souls. Many teachers bring so much more than their academic selves to the classroom
every day. But many teachers also feel overwhelmed by the obvious

need to connect with their students in ways other than scholastic. And the education system has failed to respond with adequate support for the type of professional development that is required to help teachers create the environment in which academic success is possible. A 2019 *Education Week* poll found that 76 percent of educators want more professional development in fostering students' sense of belonging in the classroom, and 41 percent of educators find it challenging or very challenging to address "the concerns of students who feel that they might be judged negatively based on their identity" (Blad, 2017, para. 4).

It's not that positive relationships between teachers and students don't happen in schools; it's just that they mostly come about accidentally. And for children of color, these relationships are less common. This is because both parties, the teacher and the student, enter the classroom with suspicions and fears generated by the same stereotypes. But these relationships do not need to be left to chance. The success of the Innocent Classroom emanates from our ability to focus on the life of each child in the classroom, one at a time; identify their good; and respond to it.

PRACTICE

- Identify three students to actively think about as we proceed.
- Think about the way each student acts in your presence, in your classroom. Think about what you know about them.
- When it is time, begin thinking about their good.

Your three students
1.
2.
3.

The natural consequence of understanding someone else's good is empathy; we cannot help but care about this person in a fundamental and essential way. And in a relationship between two people, when empathy is present, both sides feel its impact. In her talk titled "The Power of Vulnerability," author and professor Brené Brown states, "Empathy is 'feeling with' people. . . . Empathy is a choice, and it's a vulnerable choice. In order to connect with you, I need to connect with something in myself that knows that feeling" (RSA, 2013).

This is the type of relationship that is required to see a child absent of negative stereotypes and narratives. It is also the type of relationship that might give a child the chance of discarding the weight of guilt they have become accustomed to bearing. In Chapter 2, we will explore ways to recognize every child's good and build that empathetic relationship.

2 Discovering Students' Good

We have established that internalized negative stereotypes translate into a heavy burden of guilt for our children of color, and that this guilt in turn is often manifested as student disidentification from school. Ultimately, guilt raises barriers between students and teachers and obscures students' *good*. In this chapter, we'll delve deeper into ways educators can neutralize students' guilt, discover their good, and strategize ways of creating authentic relationships with them.

Neutralizing Guilt

The simple fact is, guilt hides good, so we must do our best to eliminate guilt from the classroom. In the Innocent Classroom, we work to develop our capacity to see students' destructive responses and behaviors as the result of specific internal narratives that are driven by guilt. Our job is to discover more about the way our children think about the things they think about so that we can consider their individual burdens of guilt and the ways negative stereotypes have affected their lives and ways of thinking.

Our children have a specific epistemological reality. They come from a specific family. They live on a specific street. They have a specific history. Their family history, cultural history, racial history, and economic history accumulate to a point where they see you as teacher, or they look at school, and they think something. That's epistemology: *how you think about what you think about.* It's a way of seeing things.

We each have one, too. School represents your job. Perhaps it's a place where you feel purposeful and fulfilled. Perhaps sometimes you just can't wait to leave. We can't forget that our children have a way of thinking about school that is entirely their own. Unfortunately, our epistemology and their epistemology are often in collision.

Consider the following statements:

- "I don't care."
- "It doesn't matter."
- "I don't want to."
- "What difference does it make?"

These and other negative statements are powerful indicators of a narrative infused with guilt. They denote children's surrender to the dominant negative images and definitions of themselves projected by popular culture. When a child in front of you struggles to pay attention or to care about the work you are trying to share, or is misbehaving in some form, understand that they are shackled by the negative stereotypes perpetuated about them. What you are actually witnessing is a consequence of stereotype threat: the behavior is part of a script, not a true manifestation of that child.

Children know that innocence exists, and they also know that some children are afforded its privileges. Psychologists have established that by as early as age 4, children have already learned to associate some groups with higher status, or more positive value, than others (Horwitz, Shutts, & Olson, 2014). Children of color live a constrained existence that never gets its proper sustenance.

Knowing this, we must intentionally construct strategies to address negative narratives. First, we must definitively disconnect the relationship between attitude and behavior and the narrative of guilt. There is only one healthy and viable way to do this: neutralize guilt and build innocence. This will allow us to let go of the instinct to blame families, communities, or children themselves when we are challenged by their actions (or lack thereof) and instead to focus on the derivation and detail of the narratives that cause destructive responses and behaviors. We can demonstrate a child's innocence and an understanding of their good by identifying and neutralizing each negative defining image.

The Power of Good

Disparity is the language of failed relationships. In schools, hospitals, workplaces, the legal system—in most environments where diverse groups of people depend on fair services from the institution—our inability to forge quick, authentic relationships is the source of our failure.

In the Innocent Classroom, *good* becomes the pathway to stronger and more effective relationships. People learn better from people who they believe care about them. In our work, we restate the seemingly intractable problems of race, disparity, stereotyping, and bias as a solvable question: *How does an adult (an educator) strengthen a relationship with a child (their student)?* There are three stages to this relationship-building process:

1. First, we have to believe that good exists in each of the children we work with.
2. Then, we have to believe that it is possible for us to discern the good in each of them.
3. Finally, we have to believe that responding to their good will affect their level of engagement and lead to an innocence-infused environment.

Thus, understanding good and its power to free children from their bondage to negative stereotypes is an essential pillar of the Innocent Classroom.

The Innocent Classroom's definition of *good* derives from Aristotle. In *The Nicomachean Ethics* (1996), he poses the question "What definition of the good then will hold true in all the arts?" (p. 10). His simple answer: good is "that for the sake of which all else is done" (p. 10).

I admit that I had to overcome a number of issues I had with Aristotle's known history of racism, sexism, and homophobia (Engle, 2008) to fully embrace his idea of good. In many ways, he was a blind slave to the mores of his time. Yet his distillation of good as this simple, understandable concept resonated with me. This definition of good gets at the reason why children do what they do. Why they think the way they do. Why they respond to us in a particular fashion. We can't understand these *whys* if we rely on stereotypes to discern the origin of their impulses. We must seek out children's good and help them see it so they can clear the path to its achievement.

> It changes right away, the conversation about that child. We are no longer talking about how bad the child is. We are talking about *What is the good? What is the good that we need to respond to in this child's life?*
>
> —*Constructing the Innocent Classroom participant*

Keep in mind that in the context of the Innocent Classroom, good is not the opposite of bad; it is neutral. Bank robbers rob banks because of their good. People who make a living catching bank robbers are also acting from their good. This is one of the difficulties in understanding the power of good. Educators will often say a child "has a lot of good in them" or "has a good heart," even after describing a terrible thing the child has done. This is unhelpful to understanding that child. But if we can get a handle on *why* the child acted the way they did, we are moving closer to their good. Thus, when we say, "Guilt hides good," we don't mean that students' negative behavior obscures their positive qualities, although it may; we mean that many negative behaviors are actually *manifestations* of students' hidden good.

To illustrate, a common descriptor that shows up on teachers' lists of stereotypes about students of color (see Chapter 1) is "angry." The educator who faces a seemingly inexplicably angry child might not in the moment understand that that anger may hide a variety of goods. Maybe the child never feels respected, or validated, or safe. Maybe the child doesn't feel connected to anyone or anything. Likewise, a child acting out in class is driven by something. Perhaps you have a student who takes things from their classmates. Could it be that that child is asking for your help to feel like they belong in your space? When you are feeling caught up in a child's negative behavior, ask yourself, what good is obscured by anger? By disrespect? By silence? By sadness? By argumentativeness? By bullying? By apathy? What don't you see when it seems all a child is showing is negative behavior? What is that child really asking for? What is the child really saying to you? When asked these questions, many educators respond by saying, "They just want attention," or "They want love." OK, fair enough, but those aren't precise enough to help us fashion a response to the child. *All* children want attention and love. Ask instead, *What kind of attention is the child seeking? How does that child define love?*

When a student's internalized guilt results in behaviors that inhibit your relationship development, getting to know that child's good is a powerful pathway of intervention. When you look for a child's good, you are able to see "through" their behavior or way of being. Seeing through the veil of stereotyped behaviors that a child is accustomed to showing will enable you to develop a new response to the child's behavior: inquiry rather than frustration. Developing this reflective response is one of the biggest challenges for teachers; it requires that they have the capacity, in the moment, to believe that whatever a child is doing is probably their response to an unengaged good.

This process can also give you the opportunity to help that child recover some of their authenticity. You will begin to see how rarely children of color get to act authentically, how they have been conditioned by stereotypes (and stereotype threat) to respond to all manner of things in particular ways. It is difficult to experience a child's negative behavior and simultaneously factor in the largely unknown genesis of that behavior. Knowing a child's good helps you to do so.

PRACTICE

Take a moment to write the answer to this question.

What is *your* good?

This is a good time to journal about your own sense of innocence, which we might now understand as being free of stereotypes. To help students, we must understand our own relationship to innocence and our expectations of students. Remember, you will be their coach, their lifeline . . . their baseline.

Journal about your relationship to your own sense of innocence.

The Process of Discovering Good

The following is an exchange between an elementary school educator and a trainer at one of our Innocent Classroom trainings.

> **Educator:** There's a student I'm working with who had a warm initial reaction [to my attempts to get to know him better], but then it became *Who are you? Don't talk to me.*

> **Trainer:** What is his good? This is what we're going to do in this room. You may not know yet, but eventually you'll know what good is, and you'll be able to talk about it. My first question: do you know that child's good?

Educator: I think he's an intellect.

Trainer: What does he *want?*

Educator: I don't know.

Trainer: That's a good, honest answer. Stay there. *I don't know.* And then let's find out. Who's to say that the technique you've used up till now was calibrated to what he wants? If you make a move on a child to get them to let go, and they see it as off the mark, they'll close down. It can also happen if you're right on. First, I need to know if you know his good. His intellect, his capacity, would not be it. There's something he's yearning for.

Something he's yearning for. It is easy to provide a bill of particulars regarding a child's attitude or behavior; it is more difficult to understand the world that child sees and the pressures they're under. When you look beyond the behavior, you might see one of the following yearnings behind it:

- "I can't stop feeling afraid; can you help me feel safe for a little while?"
- "I don't feel connected to anything or anybody. Can you help me feel like other people want to be around me?"
- "Can you care for me?"
- "Can you help me feel like I belong somewhere? Here, maybe?"
- "I need to be seen (or heard). Can you help me?"

These yearnings are natural and important—and often get overlooked. Thus, our realization of students' good represents a critical moment in our relationship with them. When a teacher discovers the good of a specific child—that is, *why* a child is doing whatever they are doing—they have entered into a unique relationship that that child is not expecting. *But how does one discern the good of a student?* you might ask. Indeed, this is the predominant question educators ask during discussions of good in our training sessions.

Discovering the good of a child is a journey. It can be time-consuming, because gathering information about a child is not a simple, linear process; there is no one place to find what you need in order to decisively identify that child's good. The information will probably come from multiple sources. In addition, although the good is driving the action, a child can't be expected to know that and talk about it with you. At this stage, you are as much a detective trying to solve a mystery as you are an educator, and the process will involve some guesswork.

Fortunately, knowing enough even to be able to guess at a child's good begins the transformative process. Your initial estimation of a child's good does not need to be precise. I've found that when an educator engages in the process of trying to discover good, students instinctively respond positively to the effort itself. In other words, a detective's mere attempt to search for the truth brings the truth closer. When a teacher embarks on the deliberate and intentional endeavor to know a child, the child senses it and slowly becomes more receptive to the teacher's effort. There may be resistance, but an educator's sincere effort will often overcome that resistance in even the toughest children. An educator's commitment to discover a child's good requires three things:

- **Acceptance** of a child's reality without comparison or value-based interpretations of it;
- **Vulnerability** and openness to the depth of a child's challenges; and
- **Consistency** and continual engagement even after they begin to see changes.

I know that you can find the good in each of your students and that once you find it, you can engage that good in a way that liberates the child from negative stereotypes and encourages them to show up as innocent before you. I know this because thousands of educators we have trained are currently practicing Innocent Classroom teachers, administrators, and paraprofessionals.

There is a logical, progressive series of actions you can take to understand a child's good well enough to help them feel innocent, feel lighter, and be better able to learn. You can change the classroom from a climate that accentuates the weight of guilt within children of color to one that lightens or eliminates that burden. The following sections outline the steps to discerning good.

Step 1: Observe

At the core of our effort to understand and recognize innocence and good in our students is the gathering of information that will help us see why children make the choices they do. Our goal, then, is to help children make better choices that are in line with their good and add to their capacity for innocence. Educators must strive to see who their students are, to go beyond the reputation that accompanies a child into the classroom at the beginning of the year.

Many of the children before you are largely opaque; you can't see the way they are with their friends and family or witness their lives outside school. They might live in a world of trauma or happiness, in an environment of confusion and disconnection or love and stability. Whatever the qualities of a child's life lived away from school, you can only be told of them. You must learn enough about your students to roughly calculate how these factors affect their ability to learn from you.

We sometimes get students who are kicked out of other schools within the district. I think what I've seen a shift in is that we've not judged that student based on the fact that they've gotten sent to us, but we've taken the time to sit down, get to know the student, wrap support around them from the get-go. Have conversations with them. Try to get to know them as a person rather than just a student that was kicked out of another school. And I think because of that, we are finding that a lot of these students are being more [successful], because the minute they come in they are immediately being connected with an adult who has taken the time to understand them, meet with them, let them know that they're there to support them in this transition.

—*Middle school vice principal, Providence, RI*

We must strive to see the burdens each child carries and understand the impact of negative stereotypes on their life and their outlook. We have to do our best to see precisely what a child is dealing with on a day-to-day basis. It takes time, a precious commodity, but it is an investment that will pay off royally.

During this observation step, we watch the child closely. We are noting what excites them, what may annoy them. How do they interact with other students? Who are their friends? What can you learn about their family? Pay attention to the language the child uses, the music they listen to, the movies they talk about, their heroes, what's missing in their lives. This process involves getting to know a child without being obvious about it. Gathering this information in ways that are purposeful but indirect means that the child becomes aware of your knowledge about them gradually and organically. I recommend gathering information by asking the types of questions that appear in this book's Practice sections—for example, "Whom do you admire most?" and "What don't you have that you wish you did?" I've included some examples of such questions below.

PRACTICE

What are some questions that will help you to identify a student's good?

1.	
2.	
3.	
4.	

Here are some examples:

- Name three heroes or heroines.
- Name three villains.
- What makes you happy?

- List three things that you believe in.
- List three things that you don't believe in.
- What are you an expert in?
- How many windows are in your bedroom?
- List one thing that is right and one that is wrong.
- Name one thing that is fair and one that is foul.
- Name one thing that is good and one that is bad.
- Whom would you take on your dream vacation? Why?
- Whom do you admire most?
- If you were driving and your car broke down, whom would you call?
- You get to school and find a letter on your desk. You read it and it makes you so happy. Who is it from? What does it say?

You might ask the whole class to ponder or write responses to these questions. Another approach would be to say to a student you're curious about, "A book I'm reading asked me to say whom I admire most. I chose my sister because she's persevered through a lot of bad luck. What about you? Whom do you admire?" If the child answers, you move one step closer to knowing them better. One teacher asked her 4th grade class, "How many windows are in your bedroom? Tell me when you return from recess." This question seems innocuous enough, but the results were surprisingly enlightening. When her class came back, the students gave their answers one by one: "Two, Miss." "Three, Miss." And so on. As the line shortened, she learned that some students slept in bedrooms with no windows, or in bedrooms with a lot of siblings. She also discovered that two of her students were homeless and sleeping in cars. She realized at that moment that she couldn't in good conscience teach those children the same way she did others. Understanding their good became a bit easier, as did the strategies she employed to reach them.

In short, the information you gather from observing your students, even as you academically engage them, will start to give you an idea of who they really are.

Step 2: Understand and Accept the Child's Reality

This step is performed mostly in our heads and hearts. When we have an idea about a child's daily struggles—and, let's face it, many of our children face mighty challenges every single day of their lives—the thing that is required is understanding. Not judgment or pity. This is not the time to make comparisons with ourselves, our own children, or even their classmates. It is a time to simply understand what the child is managing, coping with, or just trying to live through. What is at the source of their presentation of themselves to you?

This is a tough assignment for compassionate educators. Educators we've worked with often sense the precipice we have approached and pause at this step. It is worthy of pause, because from this step forward, we will embark on the real adventure of knowing this child's good, and there is no turning back. Why? Because the first by-product of knowing someone's good is empathy. When an educator makes an empathetic connection with a student, great things are possible, but this connection also has negative potential. It is important that the educator continuously remind themselves not to get so involved with the life of a student that they compromise their role as guide and teacher. The sadness and weight that some children carry is nearly unfathomable to us. Our job is not necessarily to rescue them from their lives; rather, by knowing and responding to a child's good, we can offer them respite from a hard life. When that child is in your class, their life has the possibility of innocence.

The challenge of knowing the details of a child's life without making value judgments is one of the hardest things many educators have to do to create an Innocent Classroom, but it is absolutely necessary. Such judgments generate feelings that distract from your goals and may inhibit a child's process of getting to trust you. This is true not only for negative value judgments but also for seemingly positive ones, like sympathy. You may feel better when you express sympathy to a child, but that sympathy offers no hope or help to them, aside from the knowledge that someone knows what is going on. We want to get deeper than that.

Step 3: Identify with Them

If step 2 is difficult, step 3 is perhaps even more so. The challenge here is to use what you've learned about each individual student to see the world around them as they do. Some teachers will admit that they have a difficult time convincing themselves that racial and cultural differences don't prevent them from being effective with many of their students. But finding a child's good demands that educators commit themselves to the journey of discovering who that child is beyond the child's behaviors and whatever stereotypes might be ascribed to them.

In order to know a child's good, we must be willing to expend the energy to understand the forces that shape that child's life. Detail isn't as important as understanding the trends, the people, and the challenges that child faces. During this step, we encourage educators to try to see the world that the child sees, to switch places with the child for a moment, to attempt to comprehend everything that impinges on the child's life. Try to avoid feeling anything judgmental, like sympathy, for that moment. Then try to see yourself through their eyes. What do you look like to them? What do you sound like to them? It isn't necessary to stay in that space very long, just long enough to understand them a bit better.

Step 4: Relate to Them

Now you have reached the point where you can build an appropriate teacher-student relationship in which each child sees you as someone who cares enough about them to teach them—and not because you are paid to do it. I have heard countless teachers talk about their heartfelt and sincere efforts to establish an effective relationship with a student, only to have the student say to them, "Yeah, right. You're paid to say that." This is why it's important not to explicitly discuss innocence in the classroom or announce the purpose behind the exercises aimed at discovering students' good. Innocence has no "street cred," so to free students from the burden of negative stereotypes, we need to use strategies that don't require us to talk about what we're doing and why we're doing it. The outcomes are based not on words but on actions: what we do and how we respond to students' good.

To support teachers' efforts in this regard, in the Innocent Classroom we have developed a list (see Figure 2.1) that reduces many behaviors, urges, and actions to their most basic impulse, or good. This guide can help drive and make specific your strategies with a student to help them begin to trust you as someone who cares.

FIGURE 2.1

How Unengaged Goods Are Manifested in the Classroom

The Good	How It's Manifested
Free	Is it possible that this child never feels like they get to make any decisions? Are they constantly being told what to do—by everybody? For this child, cumulatively, it is a triggering state of being.
Sense of belonging	Might this child feel isolated, not just from other people but also from the classroom or school environment?
Connected	Different from a sense of belonging, the good of feeling connected is predominantly about people. Is this child disconnected from their classmates?
Safe	Might this child be in a constant state of threat? Even in the "safe" environment of your class, do they still seem threatened or "unsafe"?
Cared for	Do you know of a person in this child's life who is thinking about them? Might this child be searching for someone to pay attention to them? Most educators claim that they care for their students, but do you think the child perceives your actions as signs of authentic caring?
Normal	Some children are never free of labels. More students than ever are given individualized education programs (IEPs) or greeted by new teachers who already know about their family issues, learning disabilities, and past experiences with authority or other teachers. Might this child have been bullied or always been the subject of ridicule? There are many reasons a child might feel that they are anything but normal in the context of a classroom. They may not understand that there really is no normal. Given all that, does this child need someone to help them feel free of labels?
Smart	Some children are never told they are smart, which may lead them to expect to fail or to feel frustrated with the people around them. Is this child desperate to feel that someone thinks they are smart?

The Good	How It's Manifested
Seen and heard	Children may manifest this unexpressed good in contrasting ways: some always seem to be performing, whereas others hardly speak. Some children who desire to be seen and heard exist almost invisibly; their voice is never considered. They may intentionally hide, or they may show up in a disruptive way.
Successful	Some children need to feel like they can accomplish tasks effectively. Might this child believe that no matter what they do, it never works out well? They might hesitate to demonstrate what they know or complete tasks if they don't believe they will be successful. Some students are driven to seek a feeling of success despite their own limitations. This good can generate a variety of behaviors, such as talking over other students or demonstrating cynicism about school.
Accepted	Does this child believe that who they are isn't welcomed by the people around them?
Respected	Might this child feel as though no one truly admires them for who they are or acknowledges them for what they do? Do they feel resentment toward those who seem to receive higher regard from teachers and classmates?
Untroubled	For some children, it may seem as though life offers an unending series of challenges, one after another. Is this child seeking refuge and respite from daily trauma?
Hopeful	Might this child lack any belief in a positive future? Do they live with a sense of doom and foreboding?
Validated	Many children suffer from a lack of validation from the people they most look up to. Does this child work hard to get your attention? Or have they stopped even trying to accomplish tasks after having been denied validation for so long?
Survival	Is there a sense of desperation in this child? Perhaps school and schoolwork seem superfluous in their life. For some of our children, the basic needs of survival dominate their consciousness as they try to overcome trauma and harmful circumstances. They may not know where they will end up after school or who will be there for them. This child may need you to understand their challenges and believe in their ability to overcome them.
Stable	Might this child feel shaken by a constantly changing reality outside school? Their unpredictable circumstances may prevent them from believing that stability has value. Perhaps not surprisingly, children with this good often bring confusion and chaos in their wake; stable and ordered engagement in the classroom is actually uncomfortable for them.

It is important to stress that good, in the way we have defined it here, is not just the origin of negative ways of being; it is at the core of *every* action, *every* behavior. So getting to the good of a child is a powerful tool in seeing that child as a whole person. Good generates a way of being. When we make judgments about negative and positive behavior, which we often must do, we are mostly looking at the outcome. In the Innocent Classroom, we must also uncover the behavior's origin. What is the good that caused it?

Before beginning the next Practice, let's do a walk-through. Think of a student who has caught your attention for, let's say, being disruptive in class. Now, select a good from the list in Figure 2.1. For example, maybe you choose "sense of belonging" because you've observed the student's sense of isolation or disconnection from their classmates. It's that simple: you have made your first guess about a child's good. Of course, it is only a first guess, and the more you know about that child, the more certain you might be in making your selection. But it is a beginning.

PRACTICE

With the list of three students you are thinking about from the Practice on page 33, review what you know about them. Think about how they are in class with you. What is a *good* that you think might be at the heart of each student's way of being?

Your three students	What is their good?
1.	
2.	
3.	

You might feel tempted to pick more than one good for a single student, but I don't recommend doing that. The best way to hone your skills is to focus on one good, develop strategies around that good (which we will do in Chapter 4), and evaluate the change in behavior and the quality of your relationship with that student to validate your initial choice. If there is no change in that student's behavior or your relationship with them, it is likely that the good you chose is probably not the good that lies behind the behavior. As previously noted, though, even if your guess as to a child's good is not accurate, it will lead you on a journey to know that child better. Just going to the effort is time well spent.

Embracing Good

You might suspect that some educators would think constructing an Innocent Classroom takes too much time away from academics. But in our workshops with educators, we have found that they are more likely to see the time spent as an investment rather than a cost. They are willing to invest their precious time and energy when they believe it will result in improved behavior and academic engagement. As one teacher put it, "It's not how much time you have, it's what you do with it." This sentiment was earnest, heartfelt, and, I think, persuasive to educators who were concerned about the time issue. Educators who have embraced this approach acknowledge that time is a factor but don't see it as a significant impediment. In fact, time invested up front leads to more time for high-quality instruction, because behavioral incidents and office referrals decrease when educators engage students' good.

The results speak for themselves. Among surveyed educators who completed Innocent Classroom workshops in the 2017–2018 school year, average weekly disciplinary referrals decreased by 40 percent, and 92 percent of educators observed an increase in academic mindset—that is, a child's belief of belonging in the academic community, belief in their ability to succeed, or belief that ability and competence grow with effort (Farrington et al., 2012)—when they used strategies to engage a child's good (Innocent Technologies, 2018).

When you understand the concept of children's good as the reason for which all else is done, decoding their behaviors and attitudes will present you with a real opportunity to help them embrace their own innocence—and even to educate them about this idea of good in such a way that they become advocates for their own good and begin to make choices that will lead to their own betterment and success. A big part of the Innocent Classroom is to teach our students to intervene in their own lives for their own benefit. In Chapter 3, we'll explore the valuing stage of this construction project, which includes valuing students and their innocence and helping them internalize the belief that innocence is a valuable aspect of their personality and their behavior and performance in the classroom.

3 Valuing

Once your engagement with a student has become more focused and you have begun to see their good, you have reached the next stage in our construction project: valuing. This is a very important point in the journey of creating an Innocent Classroom. When our training groups reach this stage, we feel it is a good time to think again, and in even greater depth, about the children we are focused on—and to appreciate the challenges we've already faced and the value of the potential outcomes.

Although we are not necessarily strategically acting on our growing knowledge about students and their good, this valuing occurs on multiple levels: valuing the positive changes already taking place, valuing the opportunity to forge functional relationships with students, valuing students' innocence and the time they get to be innocent in your classroom, and valuing the influence you are beginning to have with your students. Once you've taken time for this essential stage, you will be able to increase your capacity to engage with students' good.

As a result, your students will begin to feel your enhanced engagement. Innocence has been devalued in many young kids of color. Indeed, in a general sense, innocence has virtually no street credibility, which is one of the reasons we ask educators not to talk about it with their students. We want to help students internalize the belief that innocence is a valuable aspect of their personality and their behavior in the classroom without saying it directly to them. During this stage of the construction process, we begin thinking about ways of excavating and strengthening the existing manifestations of innocence demonstrated by children of color and of continuing to diminish the weight of guilt they have unwittingly accepted as theirs.

Valuing Progress, However Small

It is important to take time to reflect on and value your own work and progress as a way of renewing and reinforcing your commitment. While you are engaged in discovering each student's good, look for the small changes that are already taking place. In Innocent Classroom training sessions, we have found that many teachers progressing into the phase of strategy development don't see how their own reports about students' behavior or academic engagement have changed. To illustrate, let's look at the following scenario.

An 8th grade English teacher in an Innocent Classroom workshop brings up a student by saying,

> I'm having all kinds of problems with Elliot. He gives me nothing. I've been trying to get to know him, but he always puts on his headphones or lays his head down. I'm really frustrated. I can tell there's something in him—from some of the work he's done, I think he could be a great student—but I don't know how to reach him.

The group asks her a series of questions to see what she knows about this boy, but the teacher is genuinely flummoxed by him. He has rebuffed her every attempt to get to know him better. Then someone asks if she's aware of any of his hobbies or interests. She pauses for a moment before saying, "Yes, I guess he's really into music. I mean, I have to make him take off his headphones all the time." Someone asks her, "What's he listening to?" She has no idea. Then someone asks, "What's his good?"

How can she know his good? He won't communicate with her. She decides to use the only path available to her by committing to find out more about the music he likes.

At her next class, she asks students to write down their favorite music group or performer before they leave for the day. After reading Elliot's response, she researches the group and listens to its music. In class a few days later, during a discussion about metaphor and simile, she quotes from one of the group's songs. Although she doesn't look at Elliot, she can sense that his interest is piqued. The next day, when Elliot comes to class, he asks her if she really likes that song, and she replies that she was impressed by its use of language. She also asks him to give her some other music recommendations. From this moment, things between them begin to shift.

At the next Innocent Classroom session, though, she says she's still having trouble with Elliot doing his work on time and that he hardly participates in class discussions. Someone asks about the headphones. "Oh," she says. "Hmm. He hasn't been wearing them to class. I guess he stopped."

Another teacher asks, "Do you know what music he listens to?" She nods.

"Do you know his good?" someone asks.

She smiles. "Yes. It's 'respected.' When I show him respect, I can tell that it means something to him. I think he appreciates it."

I wanted to tell this story because teachers often miss the moment when a child is beginning to trust them. When Elliot let go of his need to block out his teacher with his headphones, the world inside that classroom changed. And I believe she almost missed it.

Valuing Students to Strengthen Relationships

If a child thinks you don't know them well enough to really care about them, they are left to express their good in their own way, which may not be healthy or productive. In constructing the Innocent Classroom, it's essential to commit to valuing your students as powerful, potentially brilliant children who are trapped in a system that does not effectively serve them. This commitment should be strengthened by the knowledge that all children have a good—no matter how they show themselves to you—and that locating their good will help you help that child.

As your relationship takes shape, it is also important to value the influence you begin to have with this child. Each child may need different aspects of your leadership to help them let go of their conditioned response to school or even to you. Remember, the reason we're doing all this is to create a relationship that that child will also value.

We must also value our students' emotional intelligence. They often know us better than we know them, and we should not assume that our good intentions translate as truth to them. Some educators are prone to speaking in platitudes when they try to motivate students, saying things like "You can be anything you want to be if you put your mind to it." Students know you have said this many times to many students. You may mean every word of it, but students won't necessarily hear it that way. Why? Because it needs a relationship to contextualize it, to make it true. Such statements of encouragement rely on facts and your direct experiences with a student to feel valid. If a child believes you truly care about them, they are much more likely to believe you mean what you say.

In the Innocent Classroom, we encourage educators to delay predictions or promises of future possibilities until they have some information about a child. Optimistic, inspirational statements can come later, when the student trusts you. When you are in the early stages of discovering good and building the relationship, it is better to stick to your process and your observations. For example, you might say, "I've been watching you, and I've noticed some interesting things about you. What if we do *X*?" And *X* is specifically based on who that child is, what that child is interested in, and why the child is acting the way they are.

Not every child will respond positively at first. Indeed, their initial reaction may be skepticism, disbelief, or even anger. But when children believe that you see and value them for who they actually are, they will allow you to prove it with a consistent focus on them—a focus they can't easily dismiss.

Valuing Students' Good to Create Empathy

Sometimes our relationships with our students are not failed but merely incomplete. When we discover, acknowledge, and value a child's good, we learn to empathize with them, and this makes the relationship complete. Simply put, good generates empathy, which increases our effectiveness with the child in front of us.

It is important to underscore here the distinction between *empathy* and *sympathy*. As discussed in Chapter 2, sympathy is the result of a value judgment and does nothing useful for its object. By contrast, the essence of empathy "is the ability to stand in another's shoes to feel what it's like there and to care about making it better if it hurts. The word itself was only coined in the early 1800s—it's a translation of the German *Einfühlung*, which means 'feeling into'" (Szalavitz & Perry, 2010, p. 13). When you empathize with someone, you are better able to see and feel the world from their perspective.

I want to offer a word of caution at this point. Educators, by nature, feel a deep connection to the struggles of the families and communities from which their students come. In our journey with these students, we are forging true empathetic connections. But we must embrace this empathy carefully. We don't want to care so much that we disregard the boundaries of the classroom. Although it is helpful to make strong connections with family and to relate a child's education to the community they are a part of, the Innocent Classroom also requires educators to limit any outside clamor that might impede a child from letting go of behaviors that are generated from negative stereotypes—after all, it is that outside noise from which many of these stereotypes originate. In addition, we can't change negative conditions such as poverty; we can only provide opportunities for a child to overcome them. We can ensure safety in the classroom, but we can't replace a parent for a child in need. In other words, our relationship with our students, although fortified with an empathetic connection, has its limits.

That said, there are times when empathy drives educators to go beyond the school walls to do the right thing, as the following vignette from one of our Innocent Classroom trainings illustrates. During this session, as we began talking about empathy, a teacher—and I think she was a good, caring teacher—raised her hand and said, "I have these kids in my class who've been itching and scratching a lot. When it gets really bad, I send them to the nurse, and she gives them some ointment. But I try not to call too much attention to how badly they seem to be itching."

I stood there as she talked, feeling increasingly uncomfortable. I didn't know what this was all about, but I could sense the rest of the room getting a little uncomfortable as well.

She continued, "I just don't want to make a big deal about it—they're Karenni kids [refugees from Myanmar]. Where they come from, this was the least of their issues. They were struggling to get here, and so I'm trying not to blow it out of proportion."

At this point, I said, "Wait. Whoa. Stop." At the same time, another teacher raised his hand and said, "I just want to say that I have had kids who have had this bedbug problem, and I went home with them and found the landlord. Then we went to health services and got the apartment cleaned up. They don't have that problem anymore."

This exchange perfectly illustrates the distinction between sympathy and empathy. The first teacher *sympathized* with her students—compassionately, yes, but she was going to let the problem continue. But the second teacher stopped it. He *empathized*.

I'm not saying every teacher can or even should follow their students home. Yet that's what needed to happen in this case. When you think about it, you know those kids will never forget: one day, they will come into full consciousness and remember that they had a teacher who cared enough to get to the root of a problem in their lives. And the sympathetic teacher's students will likewise realize one day that their teacher saw what was happening to them and didn't do anything to fix the problem. What makes it worse is realizing that the nice, sympathetic teacher was passively witnessing the creation of a potential new stereotype: *these are kids who have bedbugs.*

This story demonstrates the challenge that comes with valuing children's good and building relationships with them. This is why some educators take a step back. When we talk about creating a supportive environment for kids and building relationships with them, we ultimately arrive at this question: *Am I just going to express sympathy for my students, or am I really going to care about them?*

I've listened to a number of educators as they uncomfortably, sometimes in tears, confess that they simply don't like a specific child. Often this feeling arises after a child has lashed out at them physically, verbally, or emotionally. On occasion, a teacher's anger or dislike is accompanied by the sincere belief that their own identity, background, or set of values makes it impossible for them to understand and care about such a child.

If it is hard and painful for a teacher to express these feelings in a room full of other teachers, it is likewise difficult to hear. But when it happens, I am immediately spurred to make the case that when we engage another person's good, the first by-product is empathy. I tell teachers that we can learn to create empathy where none existed before. This assertion is often met with quiet disbelief, particularly on the part of teachers who are wounded, numb, or apathetic about the possibility of student transformation. But that is precisely the point. We must embrace disbelief to find the thing that connects us to our students. Our first reaction to a challenging situation with a student may cause us to connect to the futility of past efforts we've made with certain students. Such a challenge may trigger our instinctive reliance on the stereotypes we've been influenced by. But in the Innocent Classroom, the challenge is to reassert our disbelief in those stereotypes, or to reaffirm that our reaction to this child, at this point in our growth as an educator, requires that we not surrender to history but actually embrace a disbelief in past patterns and a renewed commitment to what lies ahead in a transformed relationship.

When we engage good, empathy follows. And from empathy grows the relationship. And from the relationship emerges a child's potential for change.

Sometimes I am tempted to say that good is the key to a child's heart, but it seems too simplistic. Yet the work to construct an Innocent Classroom, while built on a complex way of thinking about our children, yields a set of relatively simple actions born of common sense and fundamentally humanist interactions. Without empathy, this is virtually impossible. If children cannot feel our concern for their lives, it is much harder for them to believe that a virtual stranger can want what is best for them and is actively working to help them become stronger, smarter, and better able to make sense out of their world.

Increasing Our Capacity to Identify and Respond to Good

When we take on the process of creating an Innocent Classroom, it is important that we not underestimate the challenges we may encounter as we try to identify and then strategize a response to students' good. These challenges will almost necessarily involve resistance from some students, who will need time to believe that you truly care about their lives and their educational careers. It will also take time for some students to trust that they can be the energized and curious students you want them to be. Sadly, there may be some students who will simply resist any change to what is familiar to them.

So your capacity to calculate the value of your effort in relation to the impact you might have on students' lives is of great significance because you will need, at times, to replenish your commitment to them. You will need to know that the right word at the right time might change everything for them—or, more likely, that not overreacting to something they have said or done might bring your relationship into a stronger position.

As their teacher, you won't know the precise moment when your commitment to your students will change the way they see being a student in your class, but having a sense of the value you bring to their lives will increase your capacity to be ready when that moment presents itself. But it all depends on your capacity to find their good and respond to it. In the Innocent Classroom, this is the only way to reach a child's "way of being" and attempt to free them from negative ideas they hold about themselves. This is the heart of our discussion about valuing: you must find your way into the world of each and every child sitting before you in a way that may surprise both of you but that will make it possible for you guide them.

In the end, the construction of the Innocent Classroom is a challenge of conscience and commitment.

This is also a good time to check in with your own good. Understanding your own good as well as a student's enables you to approach that student knowing how closely aligned your goods are. For example, suppose your good is "validated," and you've guessed that your student's good is "belonging." You will already know that you probably won't feel validated until that child feels like they belong in your classroom or whatever space you control. Even then, they may not be able or willing to validate you, at least in the immediate future.

Your understanding of *your* good will help you understand why you might have intensely personal responses to their reactions to your attempts to build a more effective relationship with them. For example, we've found that when some teachers who see their good as "being respected" face resistance, they feel a negative personal emotional impact that gets in the way of understanding that child's good and, perhaps, the reason for their resistance. When you know your good, you can better anticipate your reactions to the students you are working with.

As you come to understand and value the good of each child under your guidance, you will begin to know them better than they ever expected you would, and better than most of the people around them.

You are not precisely trying to change their lives, here; rather, you are trying to free them from the negative stereotypes they've been ingesting virtually since their lives began. You are trying to build authentic, empathetic relationships that allow students to trust you enough to change their behavior in your classroom—for you. You are creating an environment where innocence is possible, where students believe that you care for them in a deep way.

It is important at this stage to value the time your students get to be innocent in your presence. Without explicitly discussing innocence, help them see what being innocent in your classroom offers them. Help them understand that in your class, because of who you are and the effort you've taken to know them in a way that others might not, they can be more authentic. Whatever script they follow in their lives outside your classroom, inside it, they can be free. Different. You will be there to help them understand what being free of the negative impact of stereotypes looks like, sounds like, and feels like. Once a child's good is recognized, valued, engaged, and nurtured, it becomes the path to their acceptance of their own innocence. You have the opportunity to help students see themselves differently, the way you might hope they'd see themselves. You can help change the way students envision their future selves. You can help build a narrative for them that they can buy into.

Your classroom can become the place where change begins for each child. Once your students grow to accept your guidance, you can slowly establish expectations for student performance and behavior in your room.

You are just at the beginning of your efforts to know your students well enough to begin strategizing ways to help them be their authentic, curious selves in your presence. Developing this strategic response is not a simple task, but it is doable. Before we embark on that task, let's assess your readiness. By this point in the construction process, you should know the following:

- Many of our children of color are mired in the way American culture portrays them.
- Students' response to you and to their education is often proscribed by the stereotypical images and narratives about them that they have absorbed.
- Knowing and responding to students' good increases the likelihood that they will accept you and your efforts to educate them.

At this point, you should also know how to go about identifying students' good, and you should have some idea of your current students' good.

I want to bring up again the scope of this construction project: whatever changes occur when you engage a child's good are only for you and in places you control. Strategies that work within the classroom will not necessarily work outside it. In addition, the Innocent Classroom is built one student at a time, and what works for one child will not necessarily work for another. Remember, each child has their own configuration of guilt and their own deficit of innocence. Each child deserves what you have to offer them as a unique individual.

PRACTICE

Go back to the three students you have been focusing on. For each one, take a moment to review everything you have learned. Were your guesses about each student's good accurate? Update your findings as needed. In the next chapter, we will begin to engage the goods you've identified.

Your three students	What is their good?
1.	
2.	
3.	

Sometimes our good—what's driving *us*—is not effective when responding to a child's good. Ask yourself, *How can I serve this child's good rather than my own good?*

Your three students	What is their good?	What is your good?	How can you serve the child's good?
1.			
2.			
3.			

What's interesting at this stage of our work is how the race of a child is no longer the preeminent focus; we are simply connecting with a child who has a good. This is an important moment because it validates the humanity of that child and begins to reveal their complexity. Consider the following exchange between a 9th grade teacher and a trainer at one of our Innocent Classroom trainings.

Teacher: This student is very smart, but his teachers don't treat him very nicely because he can be a daydreamer. He's been labeled as a "bad kid." He's got some stuff going on at home. His mom is very overworked, and he's become a caretaker for his other siblings. What he really wants is to be a kid. He wants to be carefree and happy. But he's growing up, and that's hard. Expectations and responsibility are hard. Him not feeling noticed is hard, too. I started working with him in middle school, and I was the only teacher he liked because I took the time to get to know him. All his other teachers called him "lazy." He's not used to people telling him he's smart or knowing that about him. Because he can be a dreamer and his mind tends to wander during class, his teachers think he's inattentive and "bad."

Trainer: What's the first thing you would do to change the direction of his life right now?

Teacher: He really loves to participate in a high-level way. For example, I would give him a word of the day, and we would review the definitions of these words. When he used the words, he'd get language-learner points that he could then trade for a sort of reward of his choice—say, he'd get to check out books that he liked or be able to write with a marker. He loves to use different media. He's very artistic, so he loves the option to use different colors and media and to incorporate movement into what he's doing. He liked the language-learner incentive system and really got into his learning, using those new vocabulary words as frequently as possible.

Trainer: Do you think he doesn't generally trust his teachers? How hard is it to get him to trust a teacher?

Teacher: It wasn't that hard because he is so used to being completely overlooked.

Trainer: Let's say that he needs to be cared for.

Teacher: I think it's carefree.

Trainer: But you want to care for him so he can be carefree, correct?

Teacher: Yes.

Trainer: I think you just gave a good tutorial on him, in terms of elevating your understanding of what he's dealing with. From that point, developing strategies that continue to challenge him is what you need to do. Challenging him publicly, in a classroom space, is OK?

Teacher: Yes, he's really smart. I did the language-learner strategy with the whole group, so it wasn't just a thing with him. Everyone had these new words to learn and then get to use.

Trainer: What about his behavior?

Teacher: If he's really invested in what he's doing and what's going on, it won't happen. He does it all year, though. He knows that in every class he can sit back and draw.

Trainer: There are students like this who are really talented. You have to find the right combination to engage their brain, and the negative behaviors will stop. By the way, we haven't mentioned the race of the children we're talking about once today. We are now at the level where we are dealing with an adult to a child, where it's just about people, their behaviors, and their realities. It's that simple, but it's informed by race and race consciousness. It's informed by the impact of racism and institutional biases. These biases are not just racial—they are also economic- and gender-based, for example. There are all kinds of biases that affect our lives and that steal our innocence away from us. But as we develop strategies for our scholars, if you feel them, their race only triggers a direction. You know what their race is, so maybe it will take you down the road to try to understand what it means to be Somali, Hmong, or Honduran, for example. Maybe it will take you down that path, and if it does, you need to go there. But you're the one who is going to make that decision.

Committing to a New Narrative

As we approach strategic engagement with students' good, it is important to remember the following:

- We now know the nature of the good of our student(s).
- We know why she doesn't smile or won't pay attention.
- We know why he has a short temper.
- We know what narrative is operating for each student.
- We know what information, images, and ideas further validate the negative stereotypes students have become accustomed to carrying.
- We know how to address students' needs better.
- We are seeing students as children who have a capacity for innocence.
- We are doing something that may impact students' lives forever.

Our job now is to value this reality in such a way that students have a chance to consider it as their own reality. Our focus will be helping students to create a new, more authentic narrative that attempts to invalidate guilt as a component of that narrative. We must be willing to experiment with new ways of presenting positive imagery and role modeling.

This is a commitment of the heart. Yes, it requires a lot from you— no question about it. But this investment will yield a return in saved time and reduced emotional distress, and it might positively change your students' lives. In the next chapter, we will begin our discussion about engaging and responding to students' good.

4 Engaging and Responding to Students' Good

Our work up to this point has been founded on the idea that children of color, through no fault of their own, suffer from a lack of innocence. At this stage of our construction project, we enter a level of interaction with our students that is based on our understanding of the importance of their innocence, and we activate our desire to dismantle the power that guilt has over them when they are in our classrooms. Thus, in this chapter, we discuss how educators can take their knowledge of a child's good and construct strategies that will respond to it.

You will notice that this chapter is structured differently from the preceding chapters, being principally composed of examples of what we call our "laboratory" work with educators. In Innocent Classroom trainings, most of our work is done in groups. Although the group process makes this work somewhat easier, individual educators can and do complete this critical phase with remarkable success. I hope that the conversations presented in this chapter shine a spotlight on the process of engaging and responding to students' good so that you will be able to turn your own observations and insights into action in your own setting—whether you are working with other educators or you are reading and thinking about the children in your class independently.

"Can't you provide a list of strategies for each good just to get me started?"

Educators commonly ask for a list or bank of strategies to try once they have discovered a child's good. But the only list that exists is the one you create between you and each individual child. Every child has their own good, and what you have learned about them will drive the ways you choose to engage that child's good. Every child is different, and even when multiple children share a good—"to be cared for," for instance—they won't necessarily benefit from the same response. For one child, to be cared for might mean regular lunch meetings where you simply provide company, whereas another child may need you to have a brush available for their hair.

You can do this. Engaging the good of individual children is a practice that you will master the more you try. And you will see that discovering and engaging students' good is itself the "best practice." Once that happens, you will find that your students are always telling you exactly what they need, and you will be able to respond to each of them more proactively, more quickly, and more focused on engaging their good.

How to Begin

Although we don't have a list of strategies, we do have a general process to respond to children's good. Pretend you are in an Innocent Classroom laboratory in which your goal is to talk about a specific student that you are having a difficult time with. You should be prepared to answer the following questions as you talk about this student. Take your time; think about the student. Think about how they think and what they could be thinking about you. Think about their life. Think about how you came to know this student. Think about their good.

- What grade is this student in?
- What age is this student?
- What do you know about this student's family?
- What do you know about how much trauma this student has experienced?

- What are some specific examples of this student's behavior and way of being in the classroom?
- What is your current relationship with this student, and how do you truly feel about them?
- What do you think is this student's good?

When you are done, review your answers. Now let's say you've chosen "validated" as a good. Give yourself some time to think about how you might provide periodic but regular validating interactions with this student. Then begin your effort.

In Innocent Classroom trainings, we frame a lab by having each group talk about a specific student. Sometimes we work with educators who come from different environments. In such cases, the educator who is talking about the child might be the only one at the table who knows them. Other times, we work with an entire faculty and staff of a school. In these situations, many people at the table are likely to know the child and can offer a more diverse set of ideas for responding to their good.

Our group lab might proceed as follows, with a 5th grade teacher talking about her student Della, whose good she has decided is "cared for."

So I don't know what's going on with Della. She's 11 and seems completely different than she has been in the past. She seems lost. Suddenly she's stopped doing homework and doesn't seem interested at all in her schoolwork. If I push her, she snaps at me. She can be really nasty. I didn't know that about her. I thought we had a great relationship, but now she won't even respond to me. I have noticed that she's not as clean and well dressed as she was in the beginning of the year. She always used to take pride in how she looked, but now it seems like she doesn't care.

I'd been thinking that something must have changed in her life, and then another teacher told me that her mother was sick. I might have heard something about that, but for some reason it never sank in. Her mother is sick. Maybe she needs to feel that someone can support her.

Put yourself in the teacher's shoes. How would you show Della that even if she thinks no one else knows what she's going through, you do? You've chosen "cared for" as her good because you think that is what is driving her behavior. And you might be right. Not only do you know her better and understand her life better, but you also are starting to care about her. But how do you let her know that you do? What are five things you can do that tell her you are there to "care for" her, that you will not watch her suffer alone?

1.

2.

3.

4.

5.

These five things will become your prescriptive response to her good. You might read a story about personal triumph in class or let her know that you know what it's like to have a parent who is ill. You might not target these actions toward her directly, but to the class in general. All you are trying to do here is to win her trust—to convince her, without saying it aloud, that she can trust you to be there and care for her.

Obviously, you need to know her well enough that the five things you wrote down will mean something to her. If you're working with colleagues in a group, they can help evaluate your strategies. For example, your groupmates may advise against reading the story but support a personal reflection, or a colleague may have an idea that is perfect for this situation.

Whether you are in a group or going about this independently, when you move to engaging good, everything you know about a child is brought to bear. There is no standard response to being "cared for." It has to come from you and your understanding of this particular child. This is why we had to disconnect from stereotypes and recognize that her behaviors—and maybe our reactions to those behaviors—were emanating from those stereotypes. Perhaps they don't necessarily represent how she actually feels.

The challenge here is to arrive at the right response to the student's good. If your identification of her good is accurate and you develop appropriate responses to that good, Della will likely change for the better. But if she doesn't begin her transformation or her behavior continues to degrade, you'll need to reevaluate your determination of her good. Maybe her good is not being "cared for"; maybe it's being "connected." Maybe she just needs someone around her whom she can talk to.

Engaging Students' Good: Examples and Practice

Now we'll move on to a series of conversations from actual Innocent Classroom training sessions that show our laboratory work in action. First, let's look at an exchange between a 7th grade teacher and an Innocent Classroom trainer.

Teacher: I have a child who is very guarded. I thought her good was accepted, but it's not accepted by adults. She doesn't want attention from me; she wants the teacher to go away.

Trainer: What are her behaviors?

Teacher: Cynical, uninterested, angry. Taunting, intimidating, competitive. She's 13 years old.

Trainer: So what is your guess about her good now, including everything you know about this child?

Teacher: Survival.

This is the moment when our work in groups begins: starting with what we know about this child and her good, every educator now has an opportunity to brainstorm with others about how this student's teacher can engage the child's good—if her good is indeed "survival"—and help her feel confident that she will make it through whatever adversity she is facing. If this child were in your class, what three ways might you try to engage her good?

1.

2.

3.

One participant in the lab might suggest reseating this student near classmates who will be accepting and supportive of her. Another educator might recommend finding times to talk to her one on one, away from the other students and about neutral topics that are unrelated to school or any stressors in her life. When the relationship is strong enough, the teacher could say to this student, "If you let me help you with some of this work, I know we can get you through this class successfully."

The following exchange between a middle school teacher and a trainer shows another example of a child with whom an educator wanted to build a relationship.

Teacher: I need help with a student. His name is José and he's an English language learner. Most of our kids are, but José has not shown growth on any of the tests. He's stayed at the same percentage. In class, he's very quiet and also very sleepy. I don't know if it's the language barrier that's keeping me from having a relationship with him, but I don't really know his good.

Trainer: What grade is he in?

Teacher: He's in 8th grade.

Trainer: OK. And you said he's quiet. What else do you think about him?

Teacher: I'd say he's afraid. Unemotional.

Trainer: What do you think this child believes that you believe about him?

Teacher: He might believe that he's invisible. Not smart. Maybe illegal, because of the language difference. He might think, *I'm legal but I don't have the language, so I don't feel like I belong.*

Trainer: We're starting to understand that we need to accept this child's view of the world. I want us to do an epistemological shift. If this child believes this is the narrative about him, what do you think he wants? What would you guess his good is?

Teacher: To fit in. To be normal.

Trainer: Let's go with that. To be normal. What can you do to help him feel normal in your classroom?

Again, I want you to think about this student. How would you help him feel normal, like he is a part of the class?

1.

2.

3.

4.

The participants in this lab suggested adding movement to the lesson plan to bring in an element of play and energy, grouping José with friends he feels comfortable with, bringing more of his language into the classroom, and even sharing some assignments with him ahead of time to give him a better shot at success, so that academic achievement can start to become part of his normal.

The following series of conversations shows more examples of educators working with one another to identify and respond to their students' goods (as opposed to their behaviors). For each example, explore responses that you think would be effective.

Here's an exchange between a high school teacher and an Innocent Classroom trainer.

> **Teacher:** I think the child I am working with in homeroom needs respect—but he has so many behaviors that I don't want to give respect to.
>
> **Trainer:** Of course. He is putting you through a gauntlet. If you survive this, he will see you as someone who gives him respect.
>
> **Teacher:** He's difficult. If I call him out on his behaviors, he will say, "Are you disrespecting me?" If I treat him in any way that doesn't feel respectful, the problems get worse.
>
> **Trainer:** And of course, that's a problem for you. You have to give him the respect anyway. For a week. If you treat him in a way that he interprets as respect, he might begin to believe you. Give it to him more. Give him opportunities so you can show him respect. And keep giving. He is going to push back and do things that will make you want to throw him out, but do it. Do it until he gives in. We want him to learn to accept your respect.

How can you show a student respect before any behaviors show up? How can you show a student respect even when they are exhibiting negative behavior? What might you do to make a student feel confident that you respect them?

1.

2.

3.

4.

The following is another exchange that shows the progress an educator made engaging his student's good.

Educator: We came to an agreement that the good of one of our most troubled students was to have that sense that someone cares for him. And over the last couple of weeks, there's been a huge amount of time put toward him and bonding with him. He used to never even be on the same side of the room as me. And yesterday, he showed up after lunch with his computer at the door. He was excited and ready to start taking the test. And he chose to sit next to me. That was a big thing, too. Because he used to book it across the room when he saw me.

Trainer: That's victory. That's huge, right? I want to pause and celebrate that. It was a ton of work, but that's a change for that child. That child has never had that connection with you, maybe with any teacher, in his entire life. And now, he at least has this feeling: *I deserve this, don't I?* Huge. And I want you to know that for the rest of this child's life, that is a permanent memory. Not just a memory, but a feeling that says, *I'm not these things. I am loved. I am cared for, for who I am. And when I feel like this, I want to show you who I really am.*

How would you demonstrate your caring for a student in your classroom?

1.

2.

3.

4.

In some cases, our own good interferes with our ability to respond to a student's good, as illustrated in the following observation from an educational equity specialist.

> I work with a teacher whose good is "connected." She is really all about connecting with her students. And she had a student whose good was "safe." And the way the teacher was trying to connect did not allow the student to feel safe. She would ask the student, "How was your weekend? Tell me about your family." And that did not make the student feel safe—to have someone, who basically represented the "government," this official, asking her about all her business.
>
> We were doing some labs as a team, and we all knew this child and realized her good was to be safe. So the teacher came up with some strategies that allowed the student to respond to some of the writing and discussion prompts through different questions, and in a way that allowed her to feel safe. The student started doing her work off to the side, and the teacher let her do that and come to her when she was ready. She created a space where the student was able to be safe. It took a little while, but they got there. And when they did, the teacher felt more connected.

What would you do to make a student in your class feel safe?

1.

2.

3.

4.

The following is an exchange between a 2nd grade dual language teacher and an Innocent Classroom trainer.

Teacher: I am suffering right now for one of my children. I feel his pain. He hates the school. It is so sad. Besides that, he's in a Spanish class and he doesn't have any interest in learning Spanish. He told me, "I don't want to be in the Spanish class. I don't want to be in the dual language program."

Trainer: What are his behaviors? How does he express his dislike?

Teacher: Sighing. He interrupts my instruction all the time. He's hyperactive. Irresponsible.

Trainer: Is he smart? Would you say he's talented academically?

Teacher: I don't know. He doesn't try.

Trainer: Is he Hispanic?

Teacher: His dad is from Mexico and speaks Spanish. Mom doesn't speak Spanish. At home they speak just English.

Trainer: There's a part of me that doesn't believe he doesn't want to be there or speak Spanish. I believe that he's said these things and acting out this way, but you understand—not trying is the script. How old is he?

Teacher: He is 7.

Trainer: So now the question is, what is his good?

Teacher: He really likes to draw.

Trainer: Be careful not to confuse his good—that for which all else is done—with something he is good at. Think about it this way: this is what I'm doing; this is why I'm doing it; this is what I want.

Teacher: Connected. His good is to be connected.

Trainer: How would you help him to feel that?

How would you help a disengaged 7-year-old student feel connected? What would you do for him?

1.

2.

3.

4.

The following exchange includes insights from a 1st grade teacher as well as the student's kindergarten teacher from the previous year.

1st grade teacher: My student was in kindergarten last year. He ended up staying half the day in preK, half the day in kindergarten, and he often slept for the first half of the day. He has a lot going on at home, a lot of behaviors at school. I taught him at summer school, and he had the same behaviors—he slept half the day, until lunch. I'm really trying to brainstorm his good right now.

Trainer: What do you know about him? Do you know what his home life is like?

Kindergarten teacher: I had him for two years. I worry about him all the time. Home life is miserable and getting worse.

1st grade teacher: Several siblings have gone through the school. There's a lot of mental health struggles and a lack of parental support at home.

Kindergarten teacher: I think his good is "seen" or "safe." Seen because he's the baby. His brothers have more concerning behaviors than he does. There have been times when he just wanted to sit on my lap and snuggle, and he's constantly looking for me toward the end of the year. When I told him he'd be in my room for the year, he came up to me and closed my computer, sat on my lap, grabbed my neck, and bawled. He always has a hand in my pocket or on my hip. But then the second that another kid looks at him or notices that, he's violent. Hitting, pushing, biting, throwing. I know they go as a family and visit one of the dads in jail. He's being exposed to situations that are confusing.

Trainer: For some of our kids, all this stuff is operating so clearly. The guilt is clear. Jail-bound; the idea that if anyone notices he's seeking some sort of comfort he lashes out—he's thinking, "I'm not supposed to want comfort." At 5 or 6 years old, he's already thinking that he doesn't deserve it, or he's not supposed to have it. When you were talking about that, I hear "cared for." When I hear about a child desperately seeking a connection with an adult, it's because they have this idea that "adults are supposed to care for me. I don't get it very often." He's also aware that there's this other way to feel cared for that he wants from you all. He's also afraid to have it. So what *could* we do, what *should* we do, what *will* we do based on all this?

What would you do to make this child feel cared for?

1.
2.
3.
4.

The next example comes from a high school English teacher who discovered her student's good over time.

Trainer: What is the good of the child you're working with?

Teacher: I believe it is feeling validated. Really and truly. Because as soon as I started to affirm what I saw in her and not let that affirmation be tainted by behavior or grades or lack of participation, that is when she started to see that her opinions and her answers are valued and matter to me, and I want her to know that. And it's when I said those types of affirmations in comparison to other affirmations that I've given, like, "I care about you" and so forth, that haven't been as successful. So I really think it comes back to being validated.

How would you validate a student?

1.

2.

3.

4.

Here's a collaborative conversation focused on a 7th grade student.

Trainer: What do you think your student's good is?

Teacher: To be accepted?

Trainer: To be accepted. Tell me why you think that.

Teacher: She has a good group of friends. I see her on the laptop with her friends. They laugh, have fun.

Trainer: What do they do?

Teacher: She's part of a group that is kind of . . . they're 7th graders, but they're still childish in a way. In a positive way. Like, they play tag with each other. So she's part of this fun little childlike group.

Trainer: Does she ever do that when she comes into your classroom?

Teacher: No. She comes in and sits down. She's quiet.

Trainer: So how can we help her feel that acceptance, what she feels with her friends, but inside the classroom?

Teacher colleague: You could think of groupwork ahead of time and place her in a group where you think she'd fit in. So she would have support, but you'd have other students in the group, too, so it's not like you're bringing extra attention to her. It would be subtle; it's almost like you have to strategize to make her feel accepted without her knowing that.

What else would you do to help this student feel accepted?

1.

2.

3.

4.

The following conversation shows how a middle school teacher and a trainer develop a likely hypothesis for a student's good.

Teacher: So Leslie is very well put together. She always looks nice. Her hair is always perfect, straight. She always plays with it during class. She has five siblings. She's the youngest, and she connects with the oldest one the best. She also has fights with her other sisters, according to her mom. Mom isn't very well put together, and she's very loud and mean to other people—to the point where she won't stop talking—versus Leslie's aunt, who is very well put together and prim and proper. Her hair is perfect, her makeup is all pretty. She sometimes comes to conferences instead of the mom.

Trainer: So you know a fair amount about Leslie. What do you think her good is?

Teacher: It's to be seen, to be validated, or to feel smart. She wants to be a surgeon. But then one day she mentioned that she could make a lot of money being a makeup artist on Instagram. She doesn't perform well in class. She's defiant and disruptive and very talkative, too.

Trainer: If you had to guess one of those three goods, what would you guess?

Teacher: I think I would guess that it's being seen.

Trainer: That makes sense to me. She's interested in pretty high-profile things—to be a surgeon, to make a lot of money, to be all over Instagram. And I trust your gut. If she's struggling and disruptive, it might be her way of sharing with you "I just want to be seen."

How can you make a child feel seen in your classroom?

1.

2.

3.

4.

Giving Students What They Need

Let's go back to the list of questions from the beginning of the chapter (pp. 68–69). Now's your chance to answer them with a specific student in mind, having read through the examples of practitioners working through the process.

PRACTICE

Select one of the students you are strengthening your relationship with and answer the following questions about them.

- What grade is this student in?
- What age is this student?
- What do you know about this student's family?
- What do you know about how much trauma this student has experienced?
- What are some specific examples of this student's behavior and way of being in the classroom?
- What is your current relationship with this student, and how do you truly feel about them?
- What do you think is this student's good?

Now, how would you engage and respond to this student's good?

1.

2.

3.

4.

Once we come to know a child's good, our job is to respond to that good—to construct new responses to the student's behavior—and give them what they are seeking. Safety. Connection. To be seen. Give to them until they look up at you in bewilderment. Until they are compelled to accept that you know who they are and what they need from you and that you might be someone who cares for them. If a student feels unsafe, they're not expecting you to care enough about them to make them feel safe all day long. But if you help them feel safe, that student is more likely to be open to you and capable of positive change.

This is what happens when educators develop responses tailored to each student's specific good.

For a while, this is all about giving. Give to them because you can, because you have the power to give and you're committed to these children. If you persist and are constant in your effort to identify a student's good and to strategize around it, you will have an impact. When students sense that you are trying to discover something about them that isn't threatening or intended to "catch" them doing something bad, they will take notice. They might not help you. They may, in fact, attempt to thwart your engagement because they won't initially believe you are trying to help them. But experience tells me that at some point, your students will open themselves to you because you are showing yourself as someone who truly understands them.

Each child in a classroom deserves this effort, although many educators begin working with students who need them the most. When you arrive at a child's good and have selected a series of actions to respond to it, you will have begun the process of offering that child a way of being innocent in your space.

As we've previously established, innocence is possible when the cumulative impact of negative stereotypes is removed or diminished in the environment you are creating for students. As you continue to focus on their good, students will gradually realize that you represent something unexpected and increasingly trustworthy. Your ability to negotiate with them will increase, as will their desire to perform more effectively in your class. They will not want to jeopardize their newfound relationship with you and will work extra hard to protect it.

In the next chapter, we focus on nurturing their innocence and maintaining the Innocent Classroom you've created.

5 Nurturing Innocence

By the time you've reached this stage in your construction project, you are aware of the way stereotypes generate negative behaviors or ways of being, you have discovered ways to see students' good and better respond to and communicate with them, and you have begun changing your students' behavior and academic mindset. Once you've strategically engaged and responded to students' good and earned a degree of trust from them, you need to nurture their burgeoning innocence. Much of this involves helping students to reacquaint themselves with innocence, reestablish its value, and recover as much of their own innocence as they can—or, for those who have managed to hold on to their innocence, to strengthen it. This chapter shares strategies to support students' understanding of how their innocence will play an important role in their success in school and to encourage them to make more decisions that are in line with their good. All these efforts are part of the ongoing management and maintenance of the Innocent Classroom that you've constructed.

What Is an Innocent Classroom?

Let's begin by revisiting what an Innocent Classroom looks like. By this point in your progression through the six stages, your classroom should be a place where

- The outside world does not intrude in a negative way.
- Students are unburdened of the weight of guilt society has imposed on them.
- Students come to know and understand their good.
- Students and their developing sense of self are supported and protected.
- You don't have to focus on the negative as a way of "keeping it real"; you can choose to let students have only innocence during the school day.
- You are free to create a new optimism based on a fundamental engagement with a student's good.
- You understand that a student's attitude or behavior is generated from their good instead of stereotypically racializing that attitude or behavior.
- Race itself is not negated or demonized but celebrated.
- Your students care about what you think of them, and you care about what your students think of you.
- Students trust you and believe that you know them and the challenges they face.
- Students come ready to learn from you—indeed, they *expect* to learn from you.

Students' journey from guilt to innocence has been traversed via the only path possible: discovering good. Engaging with students' good, gaining their trust, and helping them actualize their authentic selves constitute the soul of our work. Your classroom environment now embraces each child. You and the space you've created offer your students the chance of discovery and relevance. You can speak to students about academic subjects in a way that is contextualized by what you know about them.

Take a moment to consider one of the three students you have been focusing on. Imagine this student disconnected from the negative behaviors you might associate with them. What would that look like? Nurturing involves continually supporting students' effort to reciprocate what they now know is your heightened interest in their success. This reciprocation will come in the form of less resistant behavior and a slow but steady surrender to the belief that you actually care about them. You will have to be careful to pay attention to any small changes in their behavior in your class. What does this student need now?

As you learn more about the students in your classroom, you will have the opportunity to strengthen your connection with each of them, to help them change the way they see you, your classroom, and what you have to teach them. Students will be able to embrace their own innocence. Your knowledge and passion for teaching now have more willing and open ears. Why? Because it is you teaching them.

Nothing is more important to the lasting success of this enterprise than your effort to nourish students' sense of innocence in your classroom. To realize this goal, you might have to change every aspect of the way you interact with and evaluate each student. You might have to create new benchmarks to measure success as students make incremental progress. Remember, no matter how successful you are at identifying a student's good and developing strategies to respond to it, and no matter how well that relationship is growing, we can't expect students who have been comfortable following the old narrative to quickly transform. This is an ongoing process. Read on for how to manage and maintain the Innocent Classroom you've built.

Managing and Maintaining the Innocent Classroom

The primary focus of your work in the fledgling Innocent Classroom is finding opportunities to change students' narratives by using your knowledge of their good to provide them with regular support and sustenance. Remember, this practice requires continual empathetic interactions with your students. You can do this by providing them with validation and attempting to understand their world. Other strategies to help you manage and maintain your Innocent Classroom include tracking relationship progress, building a practice, celebrating successes, and collaborating.

Providing Validation

An effective way to strengthen relationships and nurture students' innocence is to provide them with the following two types of validation.

- **Direct and personal validation:** In previous chapters, I made a point that teachers should not explicitly talk to students about their good or the strategies being employed to build relationships. But once your relationship has taken root, you will know what you need to say to communicate to each student that you know them better than the first time they walked into your classroom. It is only natural and, I think, necessary that as you progress in developing a relationship with a student, you begin to calculate and plan specific things to say to them that will spur their personal growth and fortify your relationship. Supporting students in a general way is something that many educators are good at, and our students respond to teachers' encouragement and validation in various ways. But when an Innocent Classroom teacher who has taken the time to build a relationship offers support to a student, its significance is heightened even further. Use this opportunity to help boost a student's self-confidence and belief in their own growth.
- **Curricular validation:** You can also tailor class lectures and assignments to your students' good. For example, when you know that a particular student continually needs to be reminded that there are reasons to have hope about the future,

you can provide supplementary readings that might increase that child's capacity to believe in their own possibilities.

In the following excerpt from a training session, a teacher talks about how both forms of validation came together for her.

Teacher: When I taught summer school, we had several kids who were the "frequent fliers." There was this one kid I've known for several years. The first time I took the Innocent Classroom workshop, even at the beginning of this session, when the trainer said to write down the name of the kid whose good you have trouble seeing, it was this kid's name I wrote down. So when the kid showed up in my summer school class, I thought, *Holy moly, how am I going to get through the summer with this kid?* He's cursing. He wants to fight. He's argumentative. He's a difficult kid. If I talk to another kid about their behavior, he's the first one to step up and tell me how I'm wrong. He's really tough to deal with.

This year, his mom said, "I've had it. I need to start my life over." She left him with his dad, whom he's never lived with, and moved to Nevada to take a job.

This kid is very angry. He comes to school and he's pissed every day. So I thought, *OK, I don't know what I'm going to do, but I've had other crazy kids in the classroom. We'll figure it out.*

I decide that I'm going to teach debate to these kids because they don't want to shut up anyway. One of the Innocent Classroom workshop leaders gave me some amazing debate materials. So I presented this material to the kids, and it absolutely fascinated them. And it finally dawned on this kid, and he said, "This is what I want to do." And then I showed the kids a Bryan Stevenson TED Talk about social justice and inequity. The kids decided they wanted to debate the topic of prison reform. I said OK, and we started looking at prisons. I learned so many things that I did not want to know about for-profit prisons in America—just vile things about prison.

Of course, in debate, someone has to make the pro argument, and someone has to make the con argument. So I said to this kid, "You have to take pro and talk about for-profit prisons as a good thing." He said, "I can't do that." I said, "You've got to."

And I was able to say to him, "You know, you have a really keen sense of justice. You have a good sense of right and wrong. It's very clear that you do. And you don't think people listen. You're good at this. You could be an attorney one day. It's not about who's right or wrong; it's about who has the better argument in court. So you take pro because I already know you have strong opinions about this." This kid—he did research and looked up facts and didn't even realize he was working his butt off. I could talk to him authentically about it. And he knocked it out of the park.

So the whole time, we're building this relationship. I finally said to him, "You know what? I'm in awe of what you've been able to accomplish this summer. You're not cursing. You're not arguing. You've got presence. You've gone from wanting to yell and scream to learning how to state your opinion in a way people will hear you. I'm just so proud of you."

And he said, "Give me a piece of paper. I want you to write that down and tell me what grade I'm getting because my sperm donor [i.e., his dad] doesn't think there's one bit of good in me." I started to get big tears in my eyes, and he said, "Damn, no teacher's ever cried over me before."

Trainer: That's the point of finding [his good]. Who knew?! This is not about coddling. It's about pushing students to get them to do what they can do. The system has it messed up so bad that we can't tell what students could be good at unless we play a game with them. You focused on this child long enough to see that the way he uses language and the way his mind works go well with debate. Thank you so much for that story.

Teacher: I was lucky enough to be dealing with him. I'd previously dealt with him in a disciplinary fashion, and then I got to be his teacher. I thought this could go off the rails and suck really bad, or I could build a relationship with him and find something. I didn't know if I could do it or not.

Understanding Students' Worlds

Another aspect of maintaining the Innocent Classroom is letting your students know how much you've worked to try to understand the world they exist in. I've found that some teachers who work in challenging urban settings often don't know as much about these communities as they might. Too often, classroom discussions about community revolve around the same negative stereotypes that are perpetuated about the children of those neighborhoods. In training sessions, I sometimes talk about the importance of having a utopian mindset: when we try to prove to our students that we know about the gritty, difficult aspects of the world outside school, we inadvertently validate and reinforce those negative aspects. As a teacher of an Innocent Classroom, you can take time to acknowledge that in students' communities, there are strong, hardworking adults and families, there is faith, and there is a history that is wholly positive. Students have a chance, if they trust in their education and their relationship with you, to determine their own destiny. The more you know about the positive elements of a given community and convey that understanding to your students, the more their ability to trust and believe in you will grow.

At the same time as you understand and acknowledge students' worlds outside school, you need to continue to do your best to construct a class environment where students are free of the outside world's negative impact. Your task is to defend the boundaries of your Innocent Classroom so that your students can live through their innocence. It is understood that the outside world will always invade your classroom to some extent, but the Innocent Classroom must manifest itself more strongly than those influences. Whether you say this explicitly or more subtly telegraph it in the way you engage with your students, they will know that you are there for them and that you really care about what happens to them. This is what our children need to fortify their commitment to their own education.

Tracking Relationship Progress

The ultimate measures of success for the Innocent Classroom are improved academic achievement and increased classroom engagement. But in the beginning, progress may manifest itself differently—for example, in students being less fidgety or disruptive in your class.

These improvements stem from your new positive relationships with students. To this end, it is important to track your relationships' progress and see each relationship you have with a student as dynamic, not static. Over time, your students will be tested by all manner of challenges that may affect your relationships with them. By assessing where you are with each student on a regular basis, you will be able to evaluate the effectiveness of your attempts to engage their good. The form in Figure 5.1 shows a simple way of doing this.

This approach allows you to capture movement in your relationship. Some educators track their relationships daily; others do so on a weekly or biweekly basis. There is no single "right" way to monitor progress. Figure 5.2 (pp. 95–96) shows two forms created by educators to track their relationships with students in their own way.

Some Innocent Classroom teachers don't track in this way at all but rely on their capacity to "feel" changes and progressions in their relationships. But there is a special benefit to regularly gathering and recording this information: at a glance, it provides validation of the time and effort you've spent building relationships and presents a clear picture of students' transformation in the time they have spent with you. Once you begin charting the development of your relationship with a student, you will see exactly how your connection to this child is progressing, remains unchanged, or is degrading. I suggest keeping it simple, because you don't need another complicated form in your life. When you track progress, include the following information:

- The student's name
- The student's good
- Your strategic prescription for that student
- How you would describe your relationship with the student at the beginning of this effort
- The ways your relationship with the student is changing every day, every week, or every two weeks

FIGURE 5.1

Tracking Relationship Progress

Student Name:_____

Student's Good:_____

Opening Assessment of Relationship:　○ Excellent　○ Good　○ Not Good

Date	Strategic Prescription	Strength of Relationship
		○ Same
		○ Better
		○ Worse
		○ Same
		○ Better
		○ Worse
		○ Same
		○ Better
		○ Worse
		○ Same
		○ Better
		○ Worse

Source: Copyright 2017 Innocent Technologies, LLC. Reprinted with permission.

Students will test your commitment to them until your relationship has become a given between you. But even once a student sees this relationship as a foregone conclusion, you must try to maintain its health throughout the course of the year. This doesn't need to be taxing or time-consuming. I recommend doing the following:

FIGURE 5.2

Educator-Created Forms for Tracking Relationship Progress

Student Names	Student List						
	Good	Relationship	August	September	October	November
1. Denise	Seen	Not good	Same	Better	Better	Worse
2. Keith	Survival	Good	Worse	Worse	Same	Same
3. Lakiya	Belonging	Good	Same	Worse	Better	Worse
4. Justin	Validated	Good	Same	Better	Better	Same
5. Faith	Safe	Not good	Same	Same	Better	Better
6. Joshua	Power	Not good	Same	Same	Better	Worse
7. Anthony	Free	Good	Same	Better	Same	Same
8. Lamar	Connected	Not good	Same	Better	Better	Same
9. Ranee	Leadership	Not good	Same	Same	Better	Same
10. Tammy	Smart	Not good	Same	Same	Better	Better

Note: Students' names have been changed to protect their privacy.

Building Relationships

Month	Wendell	Emanuel	Sonya	Jacqui	Ty	Nisha	Jorge	Samuel	Rafaela	Michael	Shonna
May											
April											
March											
February											
January											
December											
November											
October											
September											
August											
Students	Wendell	Emanuel	Sonya	Jacqui	Ty	Nisha	Jorge	Samuel	Rafaela	Michael	Shonna

Note: Students' names have been changed to protect their privacy.

Key: GREAT GOOD IMPROVING BEGINNING NOT GOOD

- Be consistent with your strategies.
- Remind the student of your commitment to them.
- Keep up to date on the student's life.
- Help the student interpret the world around them in a way only you can do.
- Keep negative stereotypes and the elements that generate them out of your class.

The relationships we develop give us the ability to ask students for something personal—for example, *It breaks my heart when you use curse words in front of me.* We have to be strong enough to be vulnerable. When we know a student and have engaged their good, we might ask, "Do you see how much I care about you?"

Before you built this relationship, the student's behavior was a response to the weight of guilt they had been saddled with. When you've engaged their good in the context of an authentic relationship, their actions are no longer filtered through this guilt. Instead, the student's good will be manifested in positive behaviors, such as listening, raising their hand, trying new things, helping others, and demonstrating investment in their school. This phenomenon is depicted in what we at the Innocent Classroom call the Good Good Wheel (see Figure 5.3). We use this to illustrate the ideal impact of the Innocent Classroom. In its final, best form, the Innocent Classroom eliminates negative ways of being. This is, of course, the ideal, and perfection isn't easily achieved, but the wheel gives educators a general way to measure the impact that positive relationships have on behavior and academic mindset.

Building a Practice

More than anything, the Innocent Classroom is a practice, a muscle you must develop until it becomes second nature: you see a student and automatically ask yourself, "What is her good?" If you know her good, you'll know why she's doing what she's doing. If you don't know her good, you'll make a point to get to know her well enough to guess at it. Either way, you engage in a relationship with

FIGURE 5.3

The Good Good Wheel

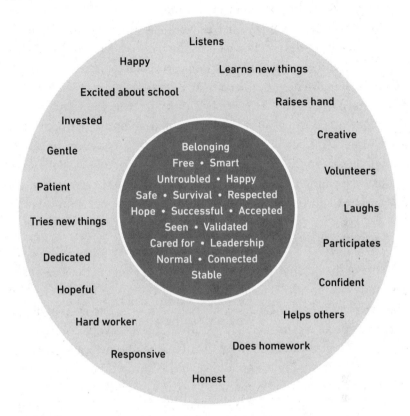

Source: Copyright 2018 Innocent Technologies, LLC. Reprinted with permission.

that student that is founded on her good. And the practice of finding and engaging good yields the kind of information that will make that engagement stronger.

When you approach this work as a practice, you will be able to take failures and disruptions in stride. You can't be put off by or quit on a student who has not responded to your effort. When you encounter a stumbling block, take a step back and reflect. Are the strategies you employed suited to engage this student's good, or should you contemplate new approaches? If you are sure that the strategies you came up with were appropriate for the good you identified, then review the information you gathered to make your initial guess at the student's good and make a new guess. Then develop new strategies and begin again with that student.

As you immerse yourself in this work—as you discover and engage this student's good, then move on to the next student, and so forth—your skills will improve. In this book, you started with 3 students. You'll build to 5. Then 10. Then all 30. Eventually, this practice will be so much a part of you that you'll be thinking about your students and their good all the time. Over time, you will develop an instinct toward good. When you begin to anticipate a student's response to certain stimuli, based on the narrative that's operating in that student's consciousness, you will think, *This child is going to have a problem with this* and be able to respond accordingly.

Celebrating Successes

One of the most difficult subjects to write about is the idea of success in the Innocent Classroom, because there will be moments of great growth and change, moments of frustration, and even moments of regression along the way. Success, in this case, is your commitment to your students, which manifests itself in a heightened radar for those who need your guidance and knowledge. If this work touches you on that level, then success is very much already in hand.

From this point, you may be bound for repeated successful moments. Every time a student quietly stops doing something that annoys you and gets in the way of their academic achievement is a success. And every time, if you are able, you should acknowledge and celebrate that success, even if it's just to yourself. As your relationship solidifies, you might also share your sense of progress with that student.

When we engage a student's good, we invite the possibility of profound change. Sometimes, these changes are small, gradual: he stays in his seat now instead of wandering the classroom; she completed a math quiz. Other times, a student's academic trajectory improves dramatically. No matter how it's measured, it's essential to recognize and celebrate growth. You regenerate your optimism by celebrating every moment of connection, every flash of innocence. If you're having trouble finding things to celebrate, look at your relationship progress tracking form. If you go too long without experiencing success, you run the risk of becoming discouraged. You have to continually build on and celebrate your successes. This has to become a habit.

Collaborating

Although each relationship you develop with a student will be unique and individual to the two of you, collaborating with colleagues to process information about students and develop strategies will expand your patience, creativity, and perspective. If you're having trouble identifying a student's good, practice doing a "lab" with a colleague and see what you come up with together. If you're stuck trying to develop a strategic response to a student whose good you are trying to engage, ask what strategies a colleague has used for other students who yearn for "safety." As you share this work with more of your fellow educators, you will harness the collective brilliance of your community of practice, providing reassurance, guidance, and celebration as each of you progresses in your relationships with students.

The Return on Investment

The Innocent Classroom process—including the effort you expend to reach every student in your classroom and to maintain that classroom, once constructed—may initially require you to spend more time performing nonacademic tasks: you have to partition the time to contemplate students' lives and to form and sustain empathetic relationships. And yes, this kind of engagement takes a fair amount of energy. Nevertheless, many educators believe that their initial investment in time and effort is returned to them over the course of a school year as discipline improves, referrals drop, and academic engagement increases. Innocent Classroom teachers tell us that although the challenge of this work may appear daunting at the beginning, as relationships develop, negative behaviors in the class decrease dramatically, as does the level of effort required to sustain the Innocent Classroom.

In the final chapter, we will talk about protecting this new environment and advocating for your students.

6   Protecting and Advocating

Your classroom is now a space where students can leave guilt at the door, where they no longer feel the threat of negative stereotypes, and where they are free to express their curiosity for learning. You now know your students better and have a deeper insight into who they are and why they perform the way they do. In this chapter, we discuss the final phase of our construction project, in which we actively guard— and help students guard—their reclaimed innocence and understanding of their own good. We consider how to sustain the work you have done and continue to do with your students, particularly as it relates to protecting and advocating for them. This protection takes on various forms, including protecting your decision to become an Innocent Classroom teacher, protecting the Innocent Classroom itself, and, above all, protecting your students—from themselves as well as from you and other adults.

Protecting your decision to become an Innocent Classroom teacher. Your commitment to the students in your class is the only thing required to be successful, but if that commitment wavers, so too will your positive impact. Thus, by maintaining your commitment to your students, you are protecting them. Your primary challenge will be to continually filter students' behaviors and attitudes through your knowledge of their good.

The simple knowledge that negative behavior, for example, has its origins in a student's good enables us to believe that we can do something to help the student show themselves differently. This can have a profound impact: you may be less likely to experience a student's behavior as an intentional statement of disrespect directed at you. Perhaps the most important aspect of being able to protect and advocate for your students has to do with how confident you are in being able to reach them. You must protect your capacity to see through behaviors without questioning your initial desire to positively influence their lives.

You decided to engage with your students, to see their good and help free them from the bondage of negative stereotypes. You will need to continuously renew this commitment so that you can protect and advocate for them. The outcome of your Innocent Classroom work was an unknown when we began, so your efforts need to be sustained by a deep belief that you can affect students' lives by engaging their good.

During a summer training session, one teacher spoke about her approach to the coming school year this way:

> From the jump, I'm going to be able to ask better questions and take more strategic steps to get to know my students that I might not have done this year. I know I tried, and the intention was there. I think I'll do better. This is a big component of it. I truly believe that those relationships have to be there first. That trust has to be there first. If you take the time to do that, good things will come.

This is the type of foundation that is required to generate the level of trust you seek with your students.

Protecting the culture of the Innocent Classroom. The classroom culture you've created doesn't allow negative stereotypes to be reinforced or even repeated. You do not let any pernicious beliefs of the outside world damage the fledgling innocence you have established. To this end, you focus on the positive, not the negative. I'm reminded of a teacher who had three boys in the back of the room who talked constantly and never paid attention. One day, the teacher pulled one of the students out of class and asked, "You play sports, right? You're on the basketball team?" When the student said he did, the teacher replied, "That's great, because I really need a leader in the back of the class. Those two guys by you aren't paying attention. I need a strong leader like you to keep them focused."

The teacher created an ally that day; his relationship with his student changed, and it reinforced the culture of his classroom. Students themselves can sense the change in the classroom when they feel that their teacher sees them more clearly and knows who they are.

Protecting students from themselves. Your students are still children. Once you have built a trusting relationship based on your understanding of students' good, you can try negotiating with them to help them see how their behavior at a given moment is not consistent with who you know them to be. They won't be able to easily dismiss your words, because they'll know that you do know them that well.

When you feel you've established a functional relationship and you experience a child who seems determined to undermine your Innocent Classroom work by reverting to their previous way of being, it can be disheartening. But it simply means you have to circle back to the strategies you've chosen to respond to their good, or you may even decide to reassess your accuracy in guessing their good. Students who have already made a big change for you will not completely abandon that relationship.

You just can't give up on them. When you feel confident that you've done the work you needed to do with a student and then the rug gets pulled out from under them in some way, you can't chalk that up as a failure. This is one of the reasons why tracking your progress with students is important: those tracking sheets provide an at-a-glance graphic of any growth or decline in your relationship. If there is a downward turn, it's probably not you but, rather, outside factors negatively affecting the student in a way that overrides everything you're doing. You must be able to step back, take credit, and celebrate what you've achieved with that student and believe that it's not completely erasable—because it's not. Remember, we started this book by saying children need to experience the feeling of innocence. And fundamentally, that's what you've been doing for them, and, by so doing, you're protecting them.

The following exchange from an Innocent Classroom training illustrates a teacher's realization of this process.

Teacher: You always want to reflect and change the way you do things. I have this one student—I have my students for two years—and to be honest, the kid drives me crazy. He just annoys me. But he is a phenomenal student, and I've tried to connect with him. I finally realized that we kind of have this battle where he doesn't shut up, and he wants my attention. I realized after meeting his parents and getting to know them better that they don't ever let him talk. So last week, I sat there with him every morning and I just let him talk. And he drove me crazy.

Trainer: Does he know he drove you crazy?

Teacher: No. He has no clue. So as the teacher, I'm like, "I'm going to find the good in every child." You know? I truly believe that you have to adapt to the children; he's not going to change who he is. So all last week, I listened to him talk all morning long until it was time for my warm-up. I got to know so much about him. And then this week, he's come in and he's just changed. But I think I changed the way I interact with him. Through innocence, I think I'm changing more than they are. It awakened me a little bit. Two years with this kid, I think I've got it. But I have changed the way I interact with him. I've had major behavior issues with him, just constant. And nothing today. Today was just a perfect day, and Friday was a perfect day. I think I connected with him. I think it just shows that we can keep evolving and improving our practice.

Protecting students from you and other adults. Understanding your own good (respect or acceptance, for example) can help you calculate your reactions to students' behavior, which is in turn generated by their own good (belonging or connectedness, for example). You want them to know that you need each and every one of them to make your class complete, and you want to make sure your class is a predictably safe place for them.

For example, you will want to let them know if you will be absent for an extended period and explain how you expect them to show the quality of your relationship to a substitute. I have been told by some teachers that the student-teacher connection in the Innocent Classroom becomes such a special one and so dependent on the teacher that, when teachers know they will be out for extended periods, they want to help their students adjust to that change in advance. When the relationship is trending strong, you may want to remind them of the journey you have taken together and how you are depending on them to carry on during your absence.

As you continue to amplify your understanding of students, you will know better how they might respond to various circumstances and be able to anticipate any challenges. You will understand the "why" of their behavior, and you will begin to form functional alliances with students. To them, you are a leader, an authority figure, to be sure, but you also want them to see you as an ally. With this status comes a responsibility to represent them as accurately as you can to your colleagues and administrators. You can use your knowledge to protect them from possibly well-meaning adults who do not understand how students' "good" may generate certain behaviors. Often, Innocent Classroom teachers feel compelled to share a student's good with another educator to explain something negative or disruptive that student has said or done. Innocent Classroom teachers feel it necessary to add a perspective that isn't totally focused on the egregious action or attitude itself. The details of a student's good do not excuse negative ways of being, but they do explain them. Innocent Classroom teachers will interrupt negative discussions about a child to ask, "Did you know that her mother is really sick and she's not being cared for very well right now?" They want, at that moment, to share something that begs for a deeper consideration of a complex child who shows up differently for them. They might also recommend a strategy that they've used that has had a positive influence.

In this way, you can change the public conversation about a child, perhaps even changing the impact of that child's difficult history before they came into your classroom. You won't be able to forget that

that child is your potentially innocent child. Their past is precisely that. With you, a new story is being written.

One of our successful Innocent Classroom teachers said in a training,

> There are young teachers in the classroom. We just got a new math teacher. I've been having a lot of the conversations that we have in [the Innocent Classroom trainings] with that young teacher. To encourage us, not just to stay with us, but to overcome some things that [challenge] a person that's not from an urban environment, just out of college, walking in. Seeing all this behavior is frightening. But when you start to talk about the sense of innocence, beauty, love . . . well. Who that person is and why they came to do the job—it's not just about the innocence of the children, but also the innocence of the teachers and staff. I think we need to encourage that more.

Journey's End

At the end of Innocent Classroom trainings, I tell participants that we've traveled over the bridge, through the forest, across the meadow, and through the hollow to get to the place where our priority is educating children. When we arrive at that spot, we are prepared to do exactly that. We've changed, and then we've tried to change the world for our children.

> **Teacher:** I have a student who was the first kid to get in trouble at our assembly at the beginning of the year. He then took it upon himself to keep that going. He's always hood up, earbuds in, I so prodded him a little bit about it. One day, he came in and had more motivation, so I asked where that was coming from, and he said, "Coach told me I need to keep my grades up so I can play." He's still struggling, trying to draw attention to himself. I think he wants to be seen.
>
> **Trainer:** Think about what happens when you give him praise. Maybe you're right about "wanting to be seen." Maybe it's something different. What grade is he in?
>
> **Teacher:** He's a sophomore.

Trainer: Don't think that just because he's a man with earphones on and he's an athlete that he doesn't need to be "cared for." Or feel like he belongs. Or seen for who he really is.

Teacher: "Seen for who he really is"—I like that. When I pull him aside and give him that praise, it feels really good. I guess it's more that he's being noticed by an adult, so "cared for" is better.

Trainer: I think it is. For many of our older kids, being safe and being cared for are critical goods that hardly ever get acknowledged. But he needs it. And you don't know the story of his life, but there's a story there. Eventually, you will know that story.

Throughout the journey, the destination wasn't really that far away. Perhaps it was just a relationship away.

Yet we've simultaneously come a long way. We began our journey by considering how marginalized children, especially children of color, are the subject of harmful stereotypes that negatively affect their ways of being. Those stereotypes work against any organic desire to show up at school and be open to learning and engaging. Of course, many of our children are ready and excited to learn, but this is *despite* the world around them portraying them in a negative light. What if the world changed and greeted our students without reinforcing those ugly stereotypes? What if our children had a teacher who spent time trying to know them and then used that knowledge as the basis for a relationship that is designed to educate them? What if?

Imagine that you could liberate children of color from negative narratives, stereotypes, and low expectations.

Imagine that you could gradually change the way these children respond to the important task you are charged with—namely, their education.

Imagine that these children could understand themselves better and value your efforts to prepare them for the challenges they face now and in the future.

Imagine these children as unburdened of the weight of guilt that forms a barrier between them and you.

Imagine them as free, if only for the hours of the school day, of the negative ideas and expectations they know exist around and about them.

Imagine, as you contemplate the nature of innocence and the good that these children possess, that you and the way you interact with them will also change for the better.

Imagine schools becoming more than safe zones, as being places that provide a strengthening sustenance that will reinforce children's best urges and instincts.

Imagine children who are able to trust you, who are able to open themselves up to the lessons you have to teach, and who are able to believe in themselves.

Imagine that, because of you, they can enter the classroom as enthusiastic, thirsty children who want to perform at their highest capacity.

Imagine that your students will learn something from you that no one ever expected they could learn—or that you could ever teach.

Imagine that this is just the beginning.

The Pledge of Innocence

It feels fitting to conclude this book with the pledge of innocence. I encourage educators to make the following pledge when they find themselves at the front of a classroom with students of color seated before them.

I pledge, as an educator of children of diverse backgrounds, races, genders, sexualities, abilities, and beliefs, that I will strive to know each child separate and apart from the stereotypes that contextualize their existence.

I pledge, upon the discovery of their good, to engage with them in such a way that their good is nourished and they are capable of showing up as innocent in my space.

Appendix: Key Terms and Definitions

Good: *That for the sake of which all else is done*

The first quality in Aristotle's definition of the hero, **good** is the thing for which everything else is done—not in the sense of "good versus bad" or "good versus evil," but why a character acts the way they do. When we know a character's good, however much we may dislike what they're doing, we will care about them because we know *why* they're doing what they're doing. We identify with the characters in *Breaking Bad* or *In Cold Blood* because we understand their good.

Good is the only path to innocence. The only way to reach a child who is infused with guilt—to get them to shed that guilt and embrace their innocence—is to identify that child's good. It takes some time for us to fully make this change in language. But trust me: in schools that go through the Innocent Classroom program, when a kid disrupts class or picks a fight, educators come together and say, "We know what the student just did; now, what's their good?"

Related to **good** is **obscured or corrupted good:** when a child's capacity to see their own good is made more difficult because of external influences and expectations.

Guilt: *The cumulative impact of negative stereotypes that affect attitude and behavior; the absence of innocence*

Guilt is more a manifestation of the negative expectations that envelop a child's life than it is a static quality. Unfortunately, most children of color are aware of this feeling at a young age and exhibit its negative consequences before they even know what is driving their behavior. Most children aren't aware that they're dragging this weight around or acting according to a toxic script that has been folded into their consciousness. They're aware that innocent people exist, that some kids don't have to deal with constant suspicion and judgment, that there's another way of being—but they are not aware that this could be *their* way of being.

Once a child internalizes stereotypes, those pernicious but formerly abstract beliefs become concrete. This might happen the first time an 8-year-old walks into Target and suddenly feels guilty about shoplifting without having done anything wrong. Guilt becomes the way our children respond to stereotypes. When they're accused of doing bad things, they think, *That's who I am.* Many children of color believe what society says about them and expect that their teachers think about them in the same way. This cumulative impact of negative stereotypes is more than a theory. It becomes a way of life, a script for living. It's weird, but it's real.

Innocence: *The condition that results from the reduction, minimization, neutralization, or elimination of the guilt that develops from stereotypes and popular negative narratives and iconography*

When was the last time you felt unburdened, free, unaffected by stereotypes and other people's opinions about you? When was the last time you could just *be?* It is essential for us as humans to know what it means to feel innocent; it is one of the most significant benchmarks in our lives.

The driving force of the Innocent Classroom's insistence on the presence of innocence in the classroom for all students, but especially for students of color, derives from the assertion that innocence, as we define it, is a fundamental quality that we must all consciously experience and understand. This experiential and theoretical understanding of innocence forms the basis of our capacity to believe in the best outcome of our actions. There is nothing that serves as a stronger quality in our endeavors than the belief that we are capable of success. Thus, our goal is to free our children from their burden of guilt and the negative scripts, to connect them directly to their good and thus to their innocence.

Educators know it's possible to develop a close, trusting relationship with a student. The educator stops looking at the student in a certain way, and the student stops seeing their teacher looking at them in that way. Educators can create an environment where they actually *see* a student, and they can reflect what they see back to that student in a way that stuns them. Schools where a sense of innocence pervades the environment generate a propulsive energy that stimulates students' desire to learn and engage.

Related to **innocence** is **innocence deficit:** the degree to which a child is incapable or unwilling to embrace their innocence.

Epistemology: *The way you think about what you think about*

All of us, including children, have our own epistemology. It's how we think about money, love, God, or food, for example. Our thinking comes from our own families, our own history.

Kids come into school with a totally different epistemology than ours. They think they know who their educators are and what their educators think about them. What do these kids see? We educators may never have imagined that. To understand students' epistemology, we must seek out information about their lives. We need to know how the student whose grandma just died, whose sibling is in jail, whose parents are going through a divorce, whose father just got laid off is thinking.

Stereotype Threat: *The fear that one's behavior may confirm or be understood in terms of a negative stereotype associated with one's social group*

Stereotype consciousness is knowledge that others endorse beliefs about the characteristics of ethnic groups. This is what we refer to as guilt, which leads to stereotype threat.

Multiple studies with minority groups confirm that stereotype threat causes a "disruptive pressure akin to anxiety," which decreases performance on achievement tests (Guyll et al., 2010). At 5 years old, children are aware that stereotypes exist. At 7, they know how to apply them.

A key way to combat this negative priming is through our relationships with children. The only way we will even get close to a true assessment of a child's ability is to help them believe that the person in that assessment process cares about them.

Empathy: *The ability to stand in another's shoes to feel what it's like there and to care about making it better if it hurts*

When you empathize with someone, you try to see and feel the world from their perspective. Your primary feelings are related more to the other person's situation than to your own. By contrast, when you sympathize, although you understand what they are going through, you don't necessarily feel it yourself. Pity similarly captures this idea of recognizing another's pain without simultaneously experiencing a sense of it oneself.

With empathy, however, you feel the other person's pain. You're feeling sorry "with" them, not just "for" them. You understand the world they come from without owning it yourself.

When an educator starts to understand a child's good, they can't help but empathize with them. The natural by-product of engaging a student's good is empathy—and empathy demands action.

References

Aristotle. (1996). *The Nicomachean ethics*. (H. Rackham, Trans.). Ware, UK: Wordsworth Editions.

Aronson, J. (2004, November). The threat of stereotype. *Educational Leadership, 62*(3), 14–19.

Bazzaz, D. (2018, November 14). Seattle Public Schools makes progress but doesn't meet most improvement goals in latest scorecard. *The Seattle Times*. Retrieved from https://www.seattletimes.com/seattle-news/education/seattle-public-schools-makes-progress-but-doesnt-meet-most-improvement-goals-in-latest-scorecard/

Blad, E. (2017, June 20). Students' sense of belonging at school is important. It starts with teachers. *Education Week*. Retrieved from https://www.edweek.org/ew/articles/2017/06/21/belonging-at-school-starts-with-teachers.html

Civic Enterprises, Bridgeland, J., Bruce, M., & Hariharan, A. (2013). *The missing piece: A national teacher survey on how social and emotional learning can empower children and transform schools*. Chicago: Collaborative for Academic, Social, and Emotional Learning. Retrieved from http://www.casel.org/wp-content/uploads/2016/01/the-missing-piece.pdf

DeGruy, J. (2005). *Post traumatic slave syndrome: America's legacy of enduring injury and healing*. Milwaukie, OR: Uptone Press.

Delpit, L. (2012). *"Multiplication is for white people": Raising expectations for other people's children*. New York: The New Press.

Du Bois, W. E. B. (1903). *The souls of black folk: Essays and sketches*. Chicago: A. C. McClurg.

Education Cities. (2016). *Education equality in America: Comparing the achievement gap across schools and cities*. Retrieved from https://files.eric.ed.gov/fulltext/ED585196.pdf

Engle, E. (2008). Aristotle, law and justice: The tragic hero. *Northern Kentucky Law Review, 35,* 1–18.

Epstein, R., Blake, J. J., & González, T. (2017). *Girlhood interrupted: The erasure of black girls' childhood.* Washington, DC: Georgetown Law, Center on Poverty and Inequality. Retrieved from https://www.law.georgetown.edu/poverty-inequality-center/wp-content/uploads/sites/14/2017/08/girlhood-interrupted.pdf

Farrington, C. A., Roderick, M., Allensworth, E., Nagaoka, J., Keyes, T. S., Johnson, D. W., et al. (2012). *Teaching adolescents to become learners. The role of noncognitive factors in shaping school performance: A critical literature review.* Chicago: University of Chicago Consortium on Chicago School Research.

Fernandez, M., & Hauser, C. (2015, September 16). Handcuffed for making clock, Ahmed Mohamed, 14, wins time with Obama. *The New York Times.* Retrieved from https://www.nytimes.com/2015/09/17/us/texas-student-is-under-police-investigation-for-building-a-clock.html

Fischer, M. J. (2010, March). A longitudinal examination of the role of stereotype threat and racial climate on college outcomes for minorities at elite institutions. *Social Psychology of Education, 13*(1), 19–40.

Gilliam, W. S., Maupin, A. N., Reyes, C. R., Accavitti, M., & Shic, F. (2016). *Do early educators' implicit biases regarding sex and race relate to behavior expectations and recommendations of preschool expulsions and suspensions?* New Haven, CT: Yale University Child Study Center. Retrieved from https://medicine.yale.edu/childstudy/zigler/publications/Preschool%20Implicit%20Bias%20Policy%20Brief_final_9_26_276766_5379_v1.pdf

Goff, P. A., Jackson, M. C., Di Leone, B. A. L., Culotta, C. M., & DiTomasso, N. A. (2014). The essence of innocence: Consequences of dehumanizing black children. *Journal of Personality and Social Psychology, 106*(4), 526–545.

Greenwald, A. G., McGhee, D. E., & Schwartz, J. L. K. (1998). Measuring individual differences in implicit cognition: The Implicit Association Test. *Journal of Personality and Social Psychology, 74*(6), 1464–1480.

Greenwald, A. G., Poehlman, T. A., Uhlmann, E., & Banaji, M. R. (2009). Understanding and using the Implicit Association Test: III. Meta-analysis of predictive validity. *Journal of Personality and Social Psychology, 97,* 17–41.

Guyll, M., Madon, S., Prieto, L., & Scherr, K. C. (2010). The potential roles of self-fulfilling prophecies, stigma consciousness, and stereotype threat in linking Latino/a ethnicity and educational outcomes. *Journal of Social Issues, 66*(1), 113–130. Retrieved from https://www.jariosvega.com/uploads/7/2/0/0/72008483/journalofsocialjustice3.pdf

Haney-López, I. (1996). *White by law: The legal construction of race.* New York: New York University Press.

Hattie, J. (2009). *Visible learning: A synthesis of over 800 meta-analyses relating to achievement.* New York: Routledge.

Horwitz, S. R., Shutts, K., & Olson, K. R. (2014). Social class differences produce social group preferences. *Developmental Science, 17*(6), 991–1002.

Innocent Technologies. (2018). *Constructing the Innocent Classroom post-program retrospective survey, fall 2017–summer 2018 aggregate.*

Irvine, J. J. (1986). Teacher-student interactions: Effects of student race, sex, and grade level. *Journal of Educational Psychology, 78*(1), 14–21.

Johnson, A. M., & Godsil, R. D. (2013, March). *Transforming perception: Black men and boys. Black male re-imagined II.* Perception Institute. Retrieved from http://perception.org/wp-content/uploads/2014/11/Transforming-Perception.pdf

Kang, J. (2005). Trojan horses of race. *Harvard Law Review, 118*(5), 1489–1593.

McKown, C., & Strambler, M. (2009, November–December). Developmental antecedents and social and academic consequences of stereotype-consciousness in middle childhood. *Child Development, 80*(6), 1643–1659.

McKown, C., & Weinstein, R. S. (2003, March–April). The development and consequences of stereotype consciousness in middle childhood. *Child Development, 74*(2), 498–515.

Musu-Gillette, L., de Brey, C., McFarland, J., Hussar, W., Sonnenberg, W., & Wilkinson-Flicker, S. (2017). *Status and trends in the education of racial and ethnic groups 2017* (NCES 2017-051). Washington, DC: U.S. Department of Education, National Center for Education Statistics. Retrieved from https://nces.ed.gov/pubs2017/2017051.pdf

National Center for Education Statistics. (2018). *Characteristics of public school teachers.* Retrieved from https://nces.ed.gov/programs/coe/indicator_clr.asp

New York Civil Liberties Union. (2019, March 14). NYCLU releases report analyzing NYPD stop-and-frisk data [Press release]. Retrieved from https://www.nyclu.org/en/press-releases/nyclu-releases-report-analyzing-nypd-stop-and-frisk-data

Oates, G. L. St. C. (2003). Teacher-student racial congruence, teacher perceptions, and test performance. *Social Science Quarterly, 84*(3), 508–525.

Plata, M. (2011). Cultural schemata—Yardstick for measuring others: Implications for teachers. *Journal of Instructional Psychology, 38*(2), 117–123.

Reyna, C. (2000). Lazy, dumb, or industrious: When stereotypes convey attribution information in the classroom. *Educational Psychology Review, 12*(1), 85–110.

Rhoden, S. (2017, Winter). "Trust me, you are going to college": How trust influences academic achievement in black males. *The Journal of Negro Education, 86*(1), 52–64.

The RSA. (2013, August 15). *The power of vulnerability—Brené Brown.* Retrieved from https://www.youtube.com/watch?v=sXSjc-pbXk4

Rubovits, P. C., & Maehr, M. L. (1973). Pygmalion black and white. *Journal of Personality and Social Psychology, 25*(2), 210–218.

Silver, E., Smith, M., & Nelson, B. (1995). The QUASAR project: Equity concerns meet mathematics education reform in the middle school. In W. Secada, E. Fennema, & L. Adajain (Eds.), *New directions for equity in mathematics education* (pp. 9–56). New York: Cambridge University Press.

Sobey, R. (2019, May 7). Boston Schools achievement gap remains wide along racial lines—A "troubling sign." *Boston Herald.* Retrieved from https://www.bostonherald.com/2019/05/07/boston-schools-achievement-gap-remains-wide-along-racial-lines-a-troubling-sign/

Society for Research in Child Development. (2009, November 14). Awareness of racism affects how children do socially and academically. *ScienceDaily.* Retrieved from https://www.sciencedaily.com/releases/2009/11/091113083301.htm

Sorhagen, N. S. (2013). Early teacher expectations disproportionately affect poor children's high school performance. *Journal of Educational Psychology, 105*(2), 465–477.

Spencer, S. J., Steele, C. M., & Quinn, D. M. (1999). Stereotype threat and women's math performance. *Journal of Experimental Social Psychology, 35*(1), 4–28.

Steele, C. M. (1997). A threat in the air: How stereotypes shape intellectual identity and performance. *American Psychologist, 52*(6), 613–629.

Szalavitz, M., & Perry, B. D. (2010). *Born for love: Why empathy is essential and endangered.* New York: William Morrow.

Telles, E. E., & Ortiz, V. (2008). *Generations of exclusion: Mexican Americans, assimilation, and race.* New York: Russell Sage Foundation.

Theisen-Homer, V. (2018, September 3). How can we support more empowering teacher-student relationships? [Blog post]. *Education Week.* Retrieved from https://blogs.edweek.org/edweek/learning_deeply/2018/09/how_can_we_support_more_empowering_teacher-student_relationships.html

White-Clark, R. (2005, April). Training teachers to succeed in a multicultural classroom. *Education Digest, 70*(8), 23–26.

Yeager, D. S., Purdie-Vaughns, V., Garcia, J., Apfel, N., Brzustoski, P., Master, A., et al. (2014). Breaking the cycle of mistrust: Wise interventions to provide critical feedback across the racial divide. *Journal of Experimental Psychology: General, 143*(2), 804–824.

Yeager, D. S., Purdie-Vaughns, V., Hooper, S. Y., & Cohen, G. L. (2017). Loss of institutional trust among racial and ethnic minority adolescents: A consequence of procedural injustice and a cause of life-span outcomes. *Child Development, 88*(2), 658–676.

Index

The letter *f* following a page number denotes a figure.

About the Author

Alexs Pate is the President and CEO of Innocent Technologies and the creator of the Innocent Classroom, a program for K–12 educators that aims to transform U.S. public education and end dispari- ties by closing the relationship gap between educa- tors and students of color. The Innocent Classroom has partnered with districts and schools throughout the United States, training more than 7,000 educa- tors. The success of the Innocent Classroom has led to the develop- ment of Innocent Classroom for Early Childhood Educators and Innocent Care training for healthcare professionals to build quick connections with their patients.

Alexs is the author of five novels, including the *New York Times* best seller *Amistad,* commissioned by Steven Spielberg's Dreamworks/ SKG and based on the screenplay by David Franzoni. Alexs's other nov- els are *Losing Absalom, Finding Makeba, The Multicultiboho Sideshow,* and *West of Rehoboth*. In October 2018, Alexs released his first chil- dren's book, *Being You* (Capstone Editions), which delivers a message of hope and self-discovery in a time of uncertainty in our world.

Prior to these pursuits, Alexs was a professor and teacher at Macalester College, the University of Minnesota, Naropa University, and the University of Southern Maine's Stonecoast Creative Writing Program, where he also earned an MFA.

Related ASCD Resources

At the time of publication, the following resources were available (ASCD stock numbers appear in parentheses).

Print Products

Becoming the Educator They Need: Strategies, Mindsets, and Beliefs for Supporting Male Black and Latino Students by Robert Jackson (#119010)

Building Equity: Policies and Practices to Empower All Learners by Dominique Smith, Nancy E. Frey, Ian Pumpian, and Douglas B. Fisher (#117031)

Cultural Competence Now: 56 Exercises to Help Educators Understand and Challenge Bias, Racism, and Privilege by Vernita Mayfield (#118043)

Culture, Class, and Race: Constructive Conversations That Unite and Energize Your School and Community by Brenda CampbellJones, Shannon Keeny, and Franklin CampbellJones (#118010)

Motivating Black Males to Achieve in School and in Life by Baruti K. Kafele (#109013)

Raising Black Students' Achievement Through Culturally Responsive Teaching by Johnnie McKinley (#110004)

Teaching to Empower: Taking Action to Foster Student Agency, Self-Confidence, and Collaboration by Debbie Zacarian and Michael Silverstone (#120006)

For up-to-date information about ASCD resources, go to www.ascd.org. You can search the complete archives of *Educational Leadership* at www.ascd.org/el.

DVD

Motivating Black Males to Achieve in School and in Life by Baruti Kafele (#611087)

The Sights and Sounds of Equitable Practices DVD by Edwin Lou Javius (#610013)

PD Online

Classroom Management: Building Effective Relationships, 2nd Edition (#PD11OC104S)

Embracing Diversity: A Look in the Mirror, 1st Edition by Katherine A. Checkley and Robin Porter (#PD09OC35S)

Embracing Diversity: Effective Teaching, 2nd Edition (#PD11OC123S)

Embracing Diversity: Managing Diverse Schools and Classrooms, 2nd Edition (#PD11OC124S)

ASCD myTeachSource®

Download resources from a professional learning platform with hundreds of research-based best practices and tools for your classroom at http://myteach-source.ascd.org/.

For more information, send an e-mail to member@ascd.org; call 1-800-933-2723 or 703-578-9600; send a fax to 703-575-5400; or write to Information Services, ASCD, 1703 N. Beauregard St., Alexandria, VA 22311-1714 USA.